Practice Behaviors Wor...

Understanding Generalist Practice

Karen K. Kirst-Ashman

University of Wisconsin Whitewater

Grafton H. Hull, Jr.

University of Utah

Prepared by

Vicki Vogel

University of Wisconsin Whitewater

BROOKS/COLE
CENGAGE Learning™

Australia • Brazil • Japan • Korea • Mexico • Singapore • Spain • United Kingdom • United States

For product information and technology assistance, contact us at **Cengage Learning Customer & Sales Support, 1-800-354-9706**

For permission to use material from this text or product, submit all requests online at **www.cengage.com/permissions** Further permissions questions can be emailed to **permissionrequest@cengage.com**

ISBN-13: 978-0-8400-3446-5
ISBN-10: 0-8400-3446-6

Brooks/Cole
20 Davis Drive
Belmont, CA 94002-3098
USA

Cengage Learning is a leading provider of customized learning solutions with office locations around the globe, including Singapore, the United Kingdom, Australia, Mexico, Brazil, and Japan. Locate your local office at: **www.cengage.com/global**

Cengage Learning products are represented in Canada by Nelson Education, Ltd.

To learn more about Brooks/Cole, visit **www.cengage.com/brookscole**

Purchase any of our products at your local college store or at our preferred online store **www.cengagebrain.com**

Printed in the United States of America
1 2 3 4 5 6 7 15 14 13 12 11

Contents

Empowerment Series

Dear Social Work Student,

Welcome to *Competencies/Practice Behaviors Workbook* for Kirst-Ashman/Hull's *Understanding Generalist Practice*, 6e. Throughout your course you will acquire a great deal of new knowledge, including an introduction to new theories, informative research, and practical skills like critical thinking skills and frameworks for appreciating and overcoming challenges. All of the knowledge you gain will offer you a deeper, richer understanding of social work. Used in conjunction with your text and other resources, the *Competencies/Practice Behaviors Workbook* presents you with Practice Exercises that will teach you how to transform your new knowledge into social work Practice Behaviors.

About Competence and Practice Behaviors

In social work, the words Competence and Practice Behavior have a unique meaning beyond the typical dictionary definitions. "Competence" in the usual sense means that a person possesses suitable skills and abilities to do a specific task. A competent baseball player must move quickly, catch, throw, and play as part of a team. They also have to think quickly, understand the rules of the game, and be knowledgeable of their environment. In the same way, a competent social worker should be able to do a number of job-related duties, think critically, and understand the context of their work. The Council on Social Work Education (CSWE) has defined specific Core Competency areas for all social work students, and their corresponding Practice Behaviors as follows:

Competencies and Practice Behaviors
2.1.1 Identify as a Professional Social Worker and Conduct Oneself Accordingly
a. Advocate for client access to the services of social work
b. Practice personal reflection and self-correction to assure continual professional development
c. Attend to professional roles and boundaries
d. Demonstrate professional demeanor in behavior, appearance, and communication
e. Engage in career-long learning
f. Use supervision and consultation
2.1.2 Apply Social Work Ethical Principles to Guide Professional Practice
a. Recognize and manage personal values in a way that allows professional values to guide practice
b. Make ethical decisions by applying standards of the National Association of Social Workers Code of Ethics and, as applicable, of the International Federation of Social Workers/ International Association of Schools of Social Work Ethics in Social Work, Statement of Principles
c. Tolerate ambiguity in resolving ethical conflicts
d. Apply strategies of ethical reasoning to arrive at principled decisions
2.1.3 Apply Critical Thinking to Inform and Communicate Professional Judgments
a. Distinguish, appraise, and integrate multiple sources of knowledge, including research-based knowledge and practice wisdom

b.	Analyze models of assessment, prevention, intervention, and evaluation
c.	Demonstrate effective oral and written communication in working with individuals, families, groups, organizations, communities, and colleagues
2.1.4	**Engage Diversity and Difference in Practice**
a.	Recognize the extent to which a culture's structures and values may oppress, marginalize, alienate, or create or enhance privilege and power
b.	Gain sufficient self-awareness to eliminate the influence of personal biases and values in working with diverse groups
c.	Recognize and communicate their understanding of the importance of difference in shaping life experiences
d.	View themselves as learners and engage those with whom they work as informants
2.1.5	**Advance Human Rights and Social and Economic Justice**
a.	Understand the forms and mechanisms of oppression and discrimination
b.	Advocate for human rights and social and economic justice
c.	Engage in practices that advance social and economic justice
2.1.6	**Engage in Research-Informed Practice and Practice-Informed Research**
a.	Use practice experience to inform scientific inquiry
b.	Use research evidence to inform practice
2.1.7	**Apply Knowledge of Human Behavior and the Social Environment**
a.	Utilize conceptual frameworks to guide the processes of assessment, intervention, and evaluation
b.	Critique and apply knowledge to understand person and environment
2.1.8	**Engage in Policy Practice to Advance Social and Economic Well-Being and to Deliver Effective Social Work Services**
a.	Analyze, formulate, and advocate for policies that advance social well-being
b.	Collaborate with colleagues and clients for effective policy action
2.1.9	**Respond to Contexts that Shape Practice**
a.	Continuously discover, appraise, and attend to changing locales, populations, scientific and technological developments, and emerging societal trends to provide relevant services
b.	Provide leadership in promoting sustainable changes in service delivery and practice to improve the quality of social services
2.1.10	**Engage, Assess, Intervene, and Evaluate with Individuals, Families, Groups, Organizations and Communities**
a.	Substantively and affectively prepare for action with individuals, families, groups, organizations, and communities
b.	Use empathy and other interpersonal skills
c.	Develop a mutually agreed-on focus of work and desired outcomes
d.	Collect, organize, and interpret client data
e.	Assess client strengths and limitations
f.	Develop mutually agreed-on intervention goals and objectives
g.	Select appropriate intervention strategies
h.	Initiate actions to achieve organizational goals
i.	Implement prevention interventions that enhance client capacities
j.	Help clients resolve problems
k.	Negotiate, mediate, and advocate for clients
l.	Facilitate transitions and endings
m.	Critically analyze, monitor, and evaluate interventions

Each of the Exercises in the *Competencies/Practice Behaviors Workbook* will focus on learning and applying social work Practice Behaviors. While every Exercise will not ask you to apply Competencies or Practice Behaviors from every Core Competency area, by the time you finish your course you will have practiced many and gained a better working knowledge of how social work is done. The goal, shared by your professors, your program, the authors of this text, and by Brooks/Cole, Cengage Learning Social Work team, is that by the end of your curriculum you will have honed your Practice Behaviors in all of the Core Competency areas into a skill set that empowers you to work effectively as a professional social worker.

Assessing Competence: Partnering with Your Instructor and Peer Evaluator
As described above, the Council on Social Work Education clearly defines the Competencies and Practice Behaviors that a social work student should be trained to employ. Therefore, the grading rubric that comes at the end of every chapter of the *Competencies/Practice Behaviors Workbook* is adapted from Competencies and Practice Behaviors defined by CSWE (see the table above). To assess your competence during your course, we recommend you partner with a peer(s) who can act as your course "evaluator(s)" to genuinely assess both your written assignments and your role-plays; be sure to ask your professor to comment on and approve the assessments once they are completed by you and your Evaluator. It is our hope that partnering with your classmates in this way will familiarize you with the unique learning opportunity you will have in your Field Experience – the signature pedagogy of social work education. There you will apply all of your knowledge and skills under the supervision of your Field Instructor and Field Liaison before completing your required curriculum.

As always, we thank you for your commitment to education and to the profession. Enjoy your course, and *feel empowered to help others*!

Chapter 1
Introducing Generalist Practice: The Generalist Intervention Model

Competencies/Practice Behaviors Exercise 1.1
Where Are You Going in Social Work?

Focus Competencies or Practice Behaviors:
- EP 2.1.1b   Practice personal reflection and self-correction to assure continual professional development

Instructions:
A.   Answer the following questions.

1.   In which areas of helping are you specifically interested (for example, adoptions, mental health, work with the older adults, alcohol and other drug abuse)? List all that you can think of. If you aren't sure or don't know as yet, say so. That's OK.

2.   Ideally, what would you like to learn from this course? Please be as specific as possible. What skills do you think you really need to learn?

3.   What are your reasons for going into social work?

4.   What practice situations do you think you might run into that scare you?

1

5. What strengths do you feel you bring to the field?

6. What weaknesses do you feel you have that might affect your work in the field?

Competencies/Practice Behaviors Exercise 1.2
What Do Social Workers Do?

Focus Competencies or Practice Behaviors:
- EP 2.1.10a Substantively and affectively prepare for action with individuals, families, groups, organizations, and communities
- EP 2.1.10g Select appropriate intervention strategies

Instructions:

A. Read chapter 1 and/or listen to your instructor's lecture concerning chapter 1 prior to beginning the exercise.

B. Read each vignette below and write possible answers to the questions following each scenario.

> **Vignette #1**
>   A fifteen-year-old can hardly make it through the morning until he can meet with his dealer and get some crack. He thinks briefly how it didn't used to be this bad, how he didn't used to "need" it this much. But he doesn't want to think about that for very long. It's too uncomfortable. He rationalizes that life is short and he wants to make the most of it. Besides, all of his friends use drugs, too. He's no different.

1. How might a social worker approach this young man regarding his drug use?

2.   What questions might you as a social worker ask?

3.   How might you encourage this young man to open up to you about his problems?

4.   What if the young man won't say anything?

5.   What if the young man expresses hostility or anger at you?

6.   What types of resources might be available to help him at the micro and mezzo levels?

3

7.   What types of programs and services at the macro level might be available?

8.   What types of programs and services might be developed at the macro level?

Vignette #2

Forlorn, homeless people are starving in the streets. Public funding for a community mental health program has been drastically cut back. That program had provided a halfway house where people could stay, receive counseling, and have their medication monitored. Years ago, the long-term, inpatient mental institution had been shut down. It was much too expensive. Now with the cutbacks, the community program can barely exist. People with serious mental and emotional problems have been turned away and are roaming the streets with nowhere to go.

---

1.   What services do you feel these people need at the micro, mezzo, and macro levels?

2.   How might you as a generalist social work practitioner go about advocating for these people? What types of social service agencies and organizations could you target for such advocacy?

3.   What programs could be developed?

4.   What are some ideas for possible funding sources?

Vignette #3

A family of four who has lived on their family farm for five generations is dispossessed. They had several bad years of crop failures and were unable to pay back the loans they so desperately needed to survive at the time. They are living in their '93 Chevy van now. They can't find any housing they could possibly afford even while working full-time, minimum-wage jobs.

1.   What services do you feel these people need at the micro, mezzo, and macro levels?

2.   How might you as a generalist social work practitioner go about advocating for these people?

5

3. What types of social service agencies and organizations could you target for such advocacy?

4. What programs could be developed?

5. What are some ideas for possible funding sources?

C. Answer the following questions about this entire exercise:

1. What was your reaction to the complexity of the problems?

2. Did this experience help you to see social work intervention in new ways? If so, in what new ways?

3.   Where did you "get stuck"? What problems seemed exceptionally difficult to solve?

4.   What skill areas do you feel you need to develop?

| **Competencies/Practice Behaviors Exercise 1.3** |
| **Change the System, Not the Person** |

Focus Competencies or Practice Behaviors:
- EP 2.1.8a   Analyze, formulate, and advocate for policies that advance social well-being
- EP 2.1.10a   Substantively and affectively prepare for action with individuals, families, groups, organizations, and communities

Instructions:
A.   Read the following three vignettes. For this exercise, do not change or move the individual. Think in terms of how the problem might be solved through macro level changes—what major organizations or community groups can do to effect change.

> **Vignette #1**
>   You are a public social services worker in a rural county. Your job includes doing everything from helping older adults obtain their social security payments to investigating alleged child abuse. Within the past six months, six farm families in the county have gone bankrupt. Government farm subsidies that used to be available have been withdrawn. It's been a bad past two years for crops. Now the banks are threatening to foreclose on the farm mortgages. Thus, the six families will literally be put out in the cold with no money and no place to go.
>   Now what?

1.   What policies might be changed?

7

2.   What community services might be developed?

3.   What might your strategies be to achieve these changes and services? (Remember, do not change the individual. Focus only on macro system change.)

Vignette #2

You are a social worker for Burp County Social Services. It's a rural county with a few towns of ten thousand people but none larger. Your job as intake worker is to do family assessments when people call up with problems (anything from domestic violence to coping with serious illnesses). Your next task is to make referrals to the appropriate services.

You have been hearing about a number of sexual assaults in the area. Women are expressing fear for their safety. People who have been assaulted don't know where to turn. The nearest large cities are over eighty miles away. You have always been interested in women's issues and advocacy for women.

Now what do you do?

1.   What policies might be changed?

2.   What community services might be developed?

3.   What might your strategies be to achieve these changes and services? (Remember, do not change the individual. Focus only on macro system change.)

Vignette #3

    You have a seventy-year-old client named Harriet living in an old, near-inner-city neighborhood in a large city. Since her husband died seven years ago, she's been living alone. She has no children. She is still in good health and likes to be independent.

    The problem is that her house has been condemned for new highway construction. The plans are to tear it down within six months. There is no public housing available for older adults within five miles of where she lives. She would like to stay in the area because she's got a lot of older adult friends there.

    Now what? (Remember, don't move Harriet.)

---

1.   What policies might be changed?

2.   What community services might be developed?

3.   What might your strategies be to achieve these changes and services? (Remember, do not change the individual. Focus only on macro system change.)

9

Focus Competencies or Practice Behaviors:

- EP 2.1.2a   Recognize and manage personal values in a way that allows professional values to guide practice
- EP 2.1.2c   Tolerate ambiguity in resolving ethical conflicts
- EP 2.1.2d   Apply strategies of ethical reasoning to arrive at principled decisions

Instructions:

A.   Make decisions regarding the following situation. How you would choose to spend the limited resources.

> You have $30,000 to spend. You must choose where it will be spent. Below are ten situations. Each situation requires spending the full amount of $30,000 in order to do any good. Dividing the money up would be useless. It would help no one.

Which of the following persons should have the $30,000 made available to help them?

a.   A premature infant (born three months early) who must be maintained in an incubator and receive medical treatment.

b.   A fifty-two-year-old man who needs a heart transplant in order to survive.

c.   A fifty-two-year-old man who needs a heart transplant in order to survive and who also happens to be your father.

d.   A five-year-old child with AIDS.

e.   You, who have graduated but have been out of work for six months.

f.   A divorced single mother with three children, a tenth-grade education, and nothing but the clothes on her back.

g.   A person with a cognitive disability who needs to live in a group home.

h.   A fourteen-year-old runaway who is addicted to cocaine and alcohol, has been prostituting herself to survive, and needs the money to enter a drug treatment program.

i.   Rehabilitation for a convicted child sexual abuser who himself was sexually abused as a child.

j.   A dispossessed urban family consisting of a couple in their late 20s and their three small children.

1.   Who should receive priority in receiving needed funds?

2.   What criteria should be used to make such decisions?

3.   What personal values did you employ in making your decision?

4.   What issues and considerations made decision making difficult?

5.   To what extent is such a decision-making situation similar to or different from situations and decisions you have encountered in real life?

6.   What could help you make such decisions more easily?

11

Competencies/Practice Behaviors Exercise 1.5
Role-Play: Understanding Systems [1]

Focus Competencies or Practice Behaviors:
- EP 2.1.7a   Utilize conceptual frameworks to guide the process of assessment, intervention, and evaluation
- EP 2.1.7b   Critique and apply knowledge to understand person and environment

Instructions:

A.   After reviewing the systems theory concepts presented in the text, role-play the following with your classmates.

B.   The family members you'll discuss are the Abbots.[2] The basic family system is pictured below. Rectangles indicate males; round-cornered rectangles indicate females. Double-pointing arrows indicate that the couple is married. Children are depicted by a vertical line descending from the arrow to their names. Dotted lines indicate relationships between people who are not married. The ages of characters follow their names. The specific characters are as follows:
- ➢ **John Abbot** and **Jill Abbot** are married. They have two children, **Ashley** and **Jack**.
- ➢ Ashley is married to **Victor Newman**. They have no children.
- ➢ Jack is married to **Nikki**. Jack and Nikki have a daughter named **Victoria**.
- ➢ Victoria is in love with **Ryan**, her boyfriend.
- ➢ **Nina**, a friend of Ryan's, really enters the picture a little later in the exercise.

C.   Have each role-player print the first name of their character on an eight-by-five-inch note card and place it in front of him or her so that observers can remember who is playing what character. The family members are to sit together inside a circle.

D.   The situations below are not sequential; each stands alone. For each situation, each member involved should be asked to respond as if he or she really was that family member. Players can add any additional details they wish about the family members they play.

---

[1] The description, objectives, and much of the procedure and commentary for this exercise are taken from "Exercise 1: The Family System" in K. Kirst-Ashman and C. Zastrow, *Student Manual of Classroom Exercises and Study Guide for Understanding Human Behavior and the Social Environment* (Chicago: Nelson-Hall, 1990).

[2] Thanks are extended here to Ruth Kirst who provided help regarding character development.

THE ABBOT FAMILY

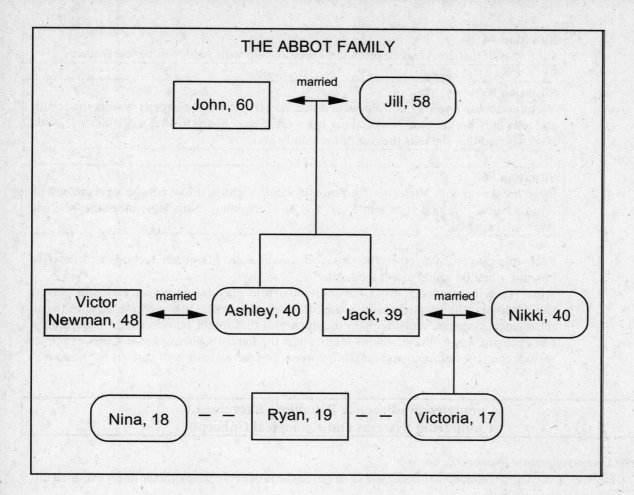

Situation #1

Jack finds out that Victor and Nikki are in love with each other. Jack is mad and moves out.

Situation #2

Victor dies of AIDS. How he contracted HIV is unknown, although Ashley suspects drug use with tainted needles. The entire family is horrified and fearful.

Situation #3

Victor is involved in the upper levels of management in DideeDry, John's paper diaper company. John owns 40 percent of the stock and is president of the company. John has a stroke and loses the use of his right side. Victor vies for control of the company. He goes to the board of directors and proposes that he take over the presidency. The board is seriously considering his request. The company needs a capable president. John is furious at Victor, as he wants to relinquish neither his control nor the presidency. John feels it will simply take some time for him to recover. Jill feels such wishful thinking is totally unrealistic.

Situation #4
Jill finds out that John had an incestuous relationship with Ashley in her early teens.

Situation #5
Victoria doubts Ryan's faithfulness and gets an HIV test. She eagerly awaits the results and tells only her mother, Nikki, about her worst fears. Much to Victoria's dismay, Nikki is so worried that she tells the rest of the family about it.

Situation #6
Ryan breaks up with Victoria. Two months later, Victoria discovers she's pregnant with Ryan's baby. Victoria runs into Ryan and Nina together. Nina announces that she and Ryan are engaged.

1. Each role player involved in the situation should share his or her feelings and describe how the situation might affect the family.

2. After receiving feedback from the individual role players, observers and role players should discuss the situation using systems theory concepts. On a separate sheet of paper, relate each systems theory term to the dynamics that might be occurring in the family. For example, any of the situations might upset the family's *homeostasis*. Other examples include the types of *input* and *output* involved, and the formation of various *subsystems*.

**Competencies/Practice Behaviors Exercise 1.6
Comparing Systems and Ecological Concepts**

Focus Competencies or Practice Behaviors:
- EP 2.1.7a Utilize conceptual frameworks to guide the process of assessment, intervention, and evaluation
- EP 2.1.7b Critique and apply knowledge to understand person and environment

Instructions:
A. After reviewing the ecological concepts presented in the text, arrange yourselves in a circle. This allows for maximum observation of the role-play activity.
B. Follow the instructions and questions presented above in Exercise 1.5, but replace ecological concepts with those of systems theory.

Chapter 1 Competencies/Practice Behaviors Exercises Assessment:

Name: _____ **Date:** _____

Supervisor's Name: _____

Focus Competencies/Practice Behaviors:

- EP 2.1.1b   Practice personal reflection and self-correction to assure continual professional development
- EP 2.1.2a   Recognize and manage personal values in a way that allows professional values to guide practice
- EP 2.1.2c   Tolerate ambiguity in resolving ethical conflicts
- EP 2.1.2d   Apply strategies of ethical reasoning to arrive at principled decisions
- EP 2.1.7a   Utilize conceptual frameworks to guide the process of assessment, intervention, and evaluation
- EP 2.1.7b   Critique and apply knowledge to understand person and environment
- EP 2.1.8a   Analyze, formulate, and advocate for policies that advance social well-being
- EP 2.1.10a   Substantively and affectively prepare for action with individuals, families, groups, organizations, and communities
- EP 2.1.10g   Select appropriate intervention strategies

Instructions:

A.   Evaluate your work or your partner's work in the Focus Competencies/Practice Behaviors by completing the Competencies/Practice Behaviors Assessment form below

B.   What other Competencies/Practice Behaviors did you use to complete these Exercises? Be sure to record them in your assessments

1.	I have attained this competency/practice behavior (in the range of 81 to 100%)
2.	I have largely attained this competency/practice behavior (in the range of 61 to 80%)
3.	I have partially attained this competency/practice behavior (in the range of 41 to 60%)
4.	I have made a little progress in attaining this competency/practice behavior (in the range of 21 to 40%)
5.	I have made almost no progress in attaining this competency/practice behavior (in the range of 0 to 20%)

EPAS 2008 Core Competencies & Core Practice Behaviors	Student Self Assessment						Evaluator Feedback
Student and Evaluator Assessment Scale and Comments	0	1	2	3	4	5	**Agree/Disagree/Comments**
EP 2.1.1 Identify as a Professional Social Worker and Conduct Oneself Accordingly:							
a. Advocate for client access to the services of social work							
b. Practice personal reflection and self-correction to assure continual professional development							
c. Attend to professional roles and boundaries							
d. Demonstrate professional demeanor in behavior, appearance, and communication							
e. Engage in career-long learning							
f. Use supervision and consultation							
EP 2.1.2 Apply Social Work Ethical Principles to Guide Professional Practice:							
a. Recognize and manage personal values in a way that allows professional values to guide practice							
b. Make ethical decisions by applying NASW Code of Ethics and, as applicable, of the IFSW/IASSW Ethics in Social Work, Statement of Principles							

15

c.	Tolerate ambiguity in resolving ethical conflicts						
d.	Apply strategies of ethical reasoning to arrive at principled decisions						
EP 2.1.3 Apply Critical Thinking to Inform and Communicate Professional Judgments:							
a.	Distinguish, appraise, and integrate multiple sources of knowledge, including research-based knowledge and practice wisdom						
b.	Analyze models of assessment, prevention, intervention, and evaluation						
c.	Demonstrate effective oral and written communication in working with individuals, families, groups, organizations, communities, and colleagues						
EP 2.1.4 Engage Diversity and Difference in Practice:							
a.	Recognize the extent to which a culture's structures and values may oppress, marginalize, alienate, or create or enhance privilege and power						
b.	Gain sufficient self-awareness to eliminate the influence of personal biases and values in working with diverse groups						
c.	Recognize and communicate their understanding of the importance of difference in shaping life experiences						
d.	View themselves as learners and engage those with whom they work as informants						
EP 2.1.5 Advance Human Rights and Social and Economic Justice:							
a.	Understand forms and mechanisms of oppression and discrimination						
b.	Advocate for human rights and social and economic justice						
c.	Engage in practices that advance social and economic justice						
EP 2.1.6 Engage in Research-Informed Practice and Practice-Informed Research:							
a.	Use practice experience to inform scientific inquiry						
b.	Use research evidence to inform practice						
EP 2.1.7 Apply Knowledge of Human Behavior and the Social Environment:							
a.	Utilize conceptual frameworks to guide the processes of assessment, intervention, and evaluation						
b.	Critique and apply knowledge to understand person and environment						
EP 2.1.8 Engage in Policy Practice to Advance Social and Economic Well-Being and to Deliver Effective Social Work Services:							
a.	Analyze, formulate, and advocate for policies that advance social well-being						
b.	Collaborate with colleagues and clients for effective policy action						
EP 2.1.9 Respond to Contexts that Shape Practice:							
a.	Continuously discover, appraise, and attend to changing locales, populations, scientific and technological developments, and emerging societal trends to provide relevant services						

16

b. Provide leadership in promoting sustainable changes in service delivery and practice to improve the quality of social services						
EP 2.1.10 Engage, Assess, Intervene, and Evaluate with Individuals, Families, Groups, Organizations and Communities:						
a. Substantively and affectively prepare for action with individuals, families, groups, organizations, and communities						
b. Use empathy and other interpersonal skills						
c. Develop a mutually agreed-on focus of work and desired outcomes						
d. Collect, organize, and interpret client data						
e. Assess client strengths and limitations						
f. Develop mutually agreed-on intervention goals and objectives						
g. Select appropriate intervention strategies						
h. Initiate actions to achieve organizational goals						
i. Implement prevention interventions that enhance client capacities						
j. Help clients resolve problems						
k. Negotiate, mediate, and advocate for clients						
l. Facilitate transitions and endings						
m. Critically analyze, monitor, and evaluate interventions						

Competencies/Practice Behaviors Exercise 2.1
Noting Nonverbal Behavior

Focus Competencies or Practice Behaviors:
- EP 2.1.10b   Use empathy and other interpersonal skills

Instructions:

A.   Review the material on nonverbal behavior in the text. Think of and write down a brief summary of some minor problem currently being experienced. Since you will be asked to share it, it should be something that is not too personal. For example, it might be how someone you live with doesn't pick up his or her dirty socks or insists that you do the dishes immediately after eating. It can be any small thing that annoys you.

B.   With another classmate, take turns being the talker and the observer. The talker should briefly explain to the observer the problem he or she previously wrote down. This should take approximately five minutes. The observer may ask questions of the talker for clarification. However, the talker should do the majority of the talking.

C.   While the talker is talking, the observer should write down brief notes concerning the talker's nonverbal behavior in the following three areas (for each area, a number of questions are raised to indicate some specific aspects of behavior the observer can note):

Eye Contact
- To what extent does the talker look you in the eye while explaining his or her problem?
- Does the talker appear to be comfortable in making eye contact with you, or does he or she frequently look away in a nervous gesture?
- Might there be some cultural differences between you and the talker that would affect the extent to which eye contact is appropriate?

Facial Expressions
- How would you describe the talker's facial expressions as she or he describes the problem?
- What specific facial movements indicate concern, humor, anger, embarrassment, or other emotions
- What specific facial movements seem to emphasize the points that the talker appears to feel are the most significant?

Body Positioning
- What specific aspects of the talker's body positioning indicate that she or he is tense or relaxed or somewhere in between?
- What specific aspects of the talker's body positioning indicate either a formal or informal style in presenting information?
- How tense/relaxed and formal/informal do you feel yourself as you sit there observing the talker?
- What zone of personal space exists between you and the talker?
- To what extent is this zone comfortable or uncomfortable to you under these conditions?

D.   After approximately five minutes of listening to the talker, the observer should take a few minutes to note whatever information she or he can remember about the talker's nonverbal behavior but didn't have a chance to record earlier. These notes can be rough and brief as they will only be used by the observer to give the talker feedback.

E.   The observer should now provide feedback to the talker concerning his or her nonverbal behavior. The observer should use the notes recorded during the activity's process. This should take about five minutes.

F.   Each pair should now reverse the roles of talker and observer. They should follow the same procedural steps, except that their roles are reversed.

G.   After all feedback concerning nonverbal behavior has been given, answer the following questions:

1.   What types of nonverbal behaviors in the three areas did you notice?

2.   To what aspects of nonverbal behavior, if any, did this exercise help to sensitize you?

3.   How did participating in this exercise feel?

4.   What did you learn from this exercise?

19

Competencies/Practice Behaviors Exercise 2.2
"Listen Up"

Focus Competencies or Practice Behaviors:
- EP 2.1.1b   Practice personal reflection and self-correction to assure continual professional development
- EP 2.1.10b   Use empathy and other interpersonal skills

Instructions:

A.   Take a moment to focus on some problem you have or some issue about which you have exceptionally strong feelings (for instance, a political issue or a religious stance). It's important that you select a topic about which you have strong feelings and opinions.

B.   With another classmate, take turns at being talker and listener. The first talker (Talker #1) should spend three minutes describing the problem or issue "off the top of his or her head." The listener (Listener #1) should remain completely silent. No written notes should be taken. It's important to rely on memory alone when it's time to give feedback.

C.   After three minutes are up, talkers should remain silent while listeners relate to talkers what they heard talkers say. Allot three minutes for this.

D.   At the end of this three-minute period, the talker and listener should answer the following questions. Do so silently without letting each other know what you're writing.

Questions for the Talker:

a.   To what extent did you feel the listener heard the major *intent* of what you were trying to say? (Circle a number.)

Didn't listen to me at all				Listened to me moderately well				Listened to me extremely well	
1	2	3	4	5	6	7	8	9	10

b.   To what extent do you feel that the listener heard what you had to say *with accurate detail*? (Circle a number.)

Little or no accurate detail				Moderately accurate detail				Extremely accurate detail	
1	2	3	4	5	6	7	8	9	10

c.   *What percentage of all that you said* did the listener relate back to you?
_____ %

d.   What were the *major errors and inaccuracies* evident in the listener's feedback?
_____
_____

20

> **Questions for the Listener:**
>
> a. To what extent did you feel you heard the major *intent* of what the talker was trying to say? (Circle a number.)
>
> Not at all   Moderately well   Extremely well
> 1   2   3   4   5   6   7   8   9   10
>
> b. To what extent do you feel that you heard what the talker had to say *with accurate detail*? (Circle a number.)
>
> Little or no   Moderately   Extremely
> accurate detail   accurate detail   accurate detail
> 1   2   3   4   5   6   7   8   9   10
>
> c. *What percentage of all that the talker said* did you relate back to him or her? _____ %
>
> d. What specific topics and areas did you *not understand or remember* very well?
> _____
> _____
> _____
> _____

E. Now exchange roles and repeat the steps. Because your roles are reversed, it's appropriate for you to complete the alternate talker/listener questionnaire. Once again, do so silently without showing each other what you've written.

F. You can now share with each other your results. Remember that the Talker Questionnaire for one should be contrasted with the Listener Questionnaire for the other. Between the two of you, take five to ten minutes to answer the following questions and issues:

1. To what extent did you agree in each experience that the talker's intent (that is, what the talker intended to say) coincided with the listener's impact (that is, what the listener heard)?

2. To what extent did you agree in each experience on the amount of detail that the listener actually heard?

3.   For each experience, how did your percentages compare regarding how much of what the talker said was related back by the listener?

4.   For each experience, compare and contrast the talker's perception of the listener's feedback with the listener's inability to understand or remember what the talker said.

5.   What differences did you find between what talkers said and what listeners heard?

6.   What types of information were omitted in the listeners' feedback?

7.   What thoughts and ideas did you gain from this exercise about communication and attentive listening?

Focus Competencies or Practice Behaviors:
- EP 2.1.2a   Recognize and manage personal values in a way that allows professional values to guide practice

Instructions:

A.   Complete the following *Who Are You?* questionnaire as honestly as possible. You do not need to share your answers unless you choose to. Take approximately ten to fifteen minutes to complete the questionnaire.

Who Are You?
(A Self-Exploratory Questionnaire)

1)   Complete the following four *who are you* statements. They can be adjectives, nouns, or longer statements. If you had to summarize who you are, what would you say?

   I am _____

   I am _____

   I am _____

   I am _____

2)   What adjectives would you use to describe yourself? Circle all that apply. They are in no particular order or priority. They are just meant to stimulate your thinking about yourself.

   Happy   Sad   Honest   Dishonest   Sensitive   Insensitive   Trustworthy   Untrustworthy   Caring   Uncaring   Outgoing Shy   Withdrawn   Friendly   Unfriendly   Religious   Not very religious   Nervous   Calm   Formal   Informal   Aggressive   Assertive   Timid   Confident   Careful   Careless   Not very confident   Capable   Incapable   Independent Dependent   Affectionate   Cool   Wary   Bold   Cheerful   Witty   Unassuming   Thorough   Easy-going   Determined   Clever   Responsive   Strong-minded   Weak-willed (at least sometimes)   Leisurely   Industrious   Controlled   Spontaneous   Serious   Funny   Tough   Pleasant   Daring   Eager   Efficient   Not so efficient   Artistic   Tactful   Intolerant   Vulnerable   Likable   Smart   Understanding   Impatient   Patient   Imaginative   Wordy   Concise   Open-minded   Funny   Organized   Somewhat disorganized   Conscientious   Late   Emotional   Unemotional   Open   Creative   Curious   Sincere   Precise   A little haphazard   Cooperative   Ethical   Brave   Mature   Eager   Spunky

3)   Cite your four greatest strengths. They can involve anything from personal qualities to talents to accomplishments. They don't have to be in any particular order or priority.

   Strength A _____

   Strength B _____

   Strength C _____

   Strength D _____

23

4)   Cite your four greatest weaknesses. These don't have to be in any order or priority either.

Weakness A _____

Weakness B _____

Weakness C _____

Weakness D _____

5)   How do you think your personal strengths will help you to work with clients in social work practice?

_____

_____

_____

_____

6)   What weaknesses, if any, do you think you need to work on to improve your ability to work with clients in social work practice?

_____

_____

_____

_____

_____

B.   After you've had time to complete the questionnaire, answer the following questions:

1.   In general, what types of personal qualities do you think are helpful when working with clients in social work practice?

2.   What personal strengths do you have that you think will be useful in the field?

Focus Competencies or Practice Behaviors:
- EP 2.1.10d   Collect, organize, and interpret client data

Instructions:

A.   Review the material in the text on using direct and indirect questions. Generally, direct questions are those that clearly ask for information. They usually can be identified because they end in a question mark. Indirect questions, on the other hand, ask questions more subtly. They imply a leading question, usually hidden in some direct statement.

B.   Consider the needs for information presented below. How might you phrase (1) a *direct* question, and how might you phrase (2) an *indirect* question to obtain the information? Supply these two questions for each of the following situations.

1.   What a single fifteen-year-old who is six months pregnant plans to do about her baby.

Direct question:

Indirect question:

2.   What a single, eighty-nine-year-old woman, still living in her own home but experiencing rapidly failing health, plans to do about her future.

Direct question:

Indirect question:

3.   How a recently divorced single mother plans to care for her three small children when she returns to work.

Direct question:

Indirect question:

4.   What a twenty-three-year-old man just out of prison and on probation (he had been convicted on several burglary charges) plans to do to support himself.

Direct question:

Indirect question:

5.   How much a thirty-five-year-old man convicted of drunk driving drinks.

Direct question:

Indirect question:

6.   What the financial resources are of a couple in their thirties applying to adopt a baby.

Direct question:

Indirect question:

7.   How a twelve-year-old girl with a cognitive disability (who has been designated as "mildly retarded") feels about her new special education teacher.

Direct question:

Indirect question:

8.   How many friends a shy, eight-year-old boy has in his neighborhood.

Direct question:

Indirect question:

9.   The amount of stress a fifty-three-year-old female executive is experiencing in her high-level administrative position.

Direct question:

Indirect question:

10.   How well a couple in their twenties who claim they're experiencing marital difficulties are able to communicate with each other.

Direct question:

Indirect question:

C.   Now, answer the following questions:

1.   How difficult was it to think up the questions, especially the indirect ones?

2.   How would you describe indirect questions, using your own words?

3.   What are the strengths and weaknesses of using direct and indirect questions?

4.   In what ways are indirect questions able to get at the needed information?

5.   What did you learn from participating in this exercise?

Competencies/Practice Behaviors Exercise 2.5
How to Respond to Clients

Focus Competencies or Practice Behaviors:
*   EP 2.1.10b   Use empathy and other interpersonal skills

Instructions:
A.   Review information in the text concerning interviews, especially focusing on verbal responses to clients. Make certain you understand how each type of response is defined and how they differ.
B.   Below are a number of statements typically made by clients. For each statement, write down examples of the different types of responses possible. Here is an example:

Example of client statement: "I'm so disgusted with my life!"
Possible responses:
Simple encouragement: "Mm-mm, please go on."
Rephrasing: "You're fed up with what's happening."
Reflective responding: "It seems that you are upset."
Clarification: "Do you mean that you don't like what's happening in your personal relationships?"
Interpretation: "Perhaps things are overwhelming you so that you feel trapped."

28

Providing information: "I can refer you to someone who can talk to you about your problems and, hopefully, help you resolve them."

Emphasizing clients' strengths: "It's good that you're getting in touch with your feelings and have chosen to share them with me. That's usually the first step in working problems out."

Self-disclosure: "Sometimes, I feel pretty disgusted, too."

Summarization (granted, it is pretty hard to summarize one measly line, so feel free to make up a summary): "So far we've discussed a number of your problems, including finances and relationships. You've also indicated how disgusted you are at this point."

Eliciting information—Closed question: "Have you just started to feel this way?"

Eliciting information—Open-ended question: "What are your reasons for being so disgusted?"

Client Statement #1: "I'm really worried about my mother."
Possible Responses:
Simple encouragement: _____
_____
_____

Rephrasing: _____
_____
_____

Reflective responding: _____
_____
_____

Clarification: _____
_____
_____

Interpretation: _____
_____
_____

Providing information: _____
_____
_____

Emphasizing clients' strengths: _____
_____
_____

Self-disclosure: _____
_____
_____

Summarization: _____
_____
_____
_____

Eliciting information—closed question: _____
_____
_____

Eliciting information—open-ended question: _____
_____
_____

29

Client Statement #2: "Hell's bells! I've got so much work to do that I don't know where
to start."
Possible responses:
Simple encouragement: _____

_____

Rephrasing: _____

_____

Reflective responding: _____

_____

Clarification: _____

_____

Interpretation: _____

_____

Providing information: _____

_____

Emphasizing clients' strengths: _____

_____

Self-disclosure: _____

_____

Summarization: _____

_____

Eliciting information—closed question: _____

_____

Eliciting information—open-ended question: _____

_____

Client Statement #3: "My dad beat me up last night."
Possible responses:
Simple encouragement: _____

_____

Rephrasing: _____

_____

Reflective responding: _____

_____

Clarification: _____

_____

Interpretation: _____
_____
_____

Providing information: _____
_____
_____

Emphasizing clients' strengths: _____
_____
_____

Self-disclosure: _____
_____
_____

Summarization: _____
_____
_____

Eliciting information—closed question: _____
_____
_____

Eliciting information—open-ended question: _____
_____
_____

Client Statement #4: "My little girl Grizelda is three-and-a-half, and hasn't started to walk yet."
Possible responses:
Simple encouragement: _____
_____
_____

Rephrasing: _____
_____
_____

Reflective responding: _____
_____
_____

Clarification: _____
_____
_____

Interpretation: _____
_____
_____

Providing information: _____
_____
_____

Emphasizing clients' strengths: _____
_____
_____

Self-disclosure: _____
_____
_____

Summarization: _____
_____
_____

Eliciting information—closed question: _____
_____
_____

Eliciting information—open-ended question: _____
_____
_____

Client Statement #5: "I just don't have enough money to pay the rent. What should I
      do?"
Possible responses:
Simple encouragement: _____
_____

Rephrasing: _____
_____

Reflective responding: _____
_____

Clarification: _____
_____

Interpretation: _____
_____

Providing information: _____
_____

Emphasizing clients' strengths: _____
_____

Self-disclosure: _____
_____

Summarization: _____
_____

Eliciting information—closed question: _____
_____

Eliciting information—open-ended question: _____
_____

C.   Address the following questions:

1.   Which types of response statements did you feel were the most difficult to develop?

2.   Which types of response statements were the easiest to think up?

3.   For each client statement, which types of response statements seem to fit best? For what reasons?

4.   To what extent did you feel that there was overlap among response types? Please specify exactly where you felt there was such overlap.

Focus Competencies or Practice Behaviors:
- EP 2.1.10b   Use empathy and other interpersonal skills

Instructions:
A.   Review the section on warmth and empathy discussed in the text.
B.   The instructor will read the series of case situations illustrated below, and will then ask for a volunteer to respond with an empathic response.
C.   The following are some examples of leading phrases that you can use to begin an empathic statement:

- My impression is that . . .
- It appears to me that . . .
- Is what you're saying that . . . ?
- Do I understand you correctly that . . . ?
- I'm hearing you say that . . .
- Do you mean that . . . ?
- Do you feel that . . . ?
- I feel that you . . .
- I'm getting the message that . . .
- You seem to be . . .
- When you say that, I think you . . .
- You look as if you . . .
- You sound so _____. Can we talk more about it?
- You look _____. What's been happening?

D.   Your instructor will read and ask you to respond to the five case vignettes cited below. After each case, the class can discuss the following two questions:

a.   What various responses are possible in this case situation?
b.   How do various responses compare and contrast in terms of their effectiveness?

Vignette #1
        You are a social worker in foster care. You're making a home visit to one of the foster homes on your caseload. The purpose is to talk with both foster parents and determine how things are going with their nine-year-old foster child, Katie. The couple has three children of their own, all of whom are in college. In the past the foster couple has expressed some interest in adopting Katie. When you get to the home, only the mother is present. After polite initial greetings, the foster mother states, "Katie certainly doesn't like to read very much like the rest of us. I think she gets bored when she's not doing something active. Many times I just don't know what to do with her."
        You *empathically* respond . . .   (Remember that you *do not* have to solve the problem right now. You only need to let your client know that you understand how she feels.)

Vignette #2

You are a social worker in a health care facility for the elderly. Helen is a resident who has been living there for approximately two years. All rooms have two residents, which has consistently been a problem for Helen. Her current roommate is Hilda, a quiet woman who rarely interacts with any of the other residents. Helen is very possessive of her things and wants no one else to touch them. Additionally, Helen does not like to share the bathroom, which is also used by the two residents in the next room. Helen, a strong, outspoken woman even at age ninety-seven, approaches you and states, "Hilda keeps using my bathroom and pushes my things around. I want her out of there right now! You do something right now!"

You *empathically* respond . . .

Vignette # 3

You are a school social worker. Romy, age sixteen, was in the men's bathroom when several other students were caught using drugs. Romy insists it was the others who were guilty and he was innocent. He said he just happened to be in the restroom at the same time. The teacher who found them couldn't distinguish who was guilty and who was not, so put them all on "penalty." That means detentions after school and exclusion from any sports for two weeks. Romy is furious. He comes up to you and states, "It's not fair! It's just not fair! I'm innocent and I'm getting punished anyway. I should've used the drugs if I'm going to get the punishment."

You *empathically* respond . . .

Vignette # 4

You are a social worker at a diagnostic and treatment center for children who have multiple disabilities. Your primary function is to work with parents, helping them to cope with the pressures they are under and connecting them with resources they need. A mother of a five-year-old boy with severe cerebral palsy[1] talks with you on a weekly basis. Her son has serious difficulties. He has very little muscular control. He can't walk by himself or talk, although his speech, occupational, and physical therapists feel he has normal intelligence. The mother's husband is of a religion that denies the existence of disease and of physical impairment. Thus, he denies that his son has a disability. The burden of caregiving rests solely upon the mother. She loves her son dearly and generally does what she can for him enthusiastically. She enters your office one day, says hello, and sits down. She immediately puts her hand to her eyes and breaks down in tears.

You *empathically* respond . . .

---

[1] *Cerebral palsy* is a condition of the brain that results from damage before or during birth. Symptoms include difficulties in speech and mobility.

Focus Competencies or Practice Behaviors:
- EP 2.1.10a   Substantively and affectively prepare for action with individuals, families, groups, organizations, and communities
- EP 2.1.10b   Use empathy and other interpersonal skills

Instructions:

A.   Review the material on interviewing, especially that on silence in the interview and on doing the interview which is discussed in the text. It is also helpful to review related material on breast cancer, on HIV/AIDS, and on dealing with grief prior to undertaking the respective role play.[2]

B.   After reading one of the following three client scenarios, the instructor will ask for a volunteer to play the role before the class. The volunteer will sit in the front of the class and respond as if she or he was the client.

To avoid placing full responsibility for the social work role on any one individual, the worker role will be assumed on a general basis by the remainder of the class. Volunteers may jump in with responses they feel are appropriate. In the event that more than one person responds at the same time, the instructor will monitor the progression of turns.

Role-Play A: Silence and Breast Cancer

Client Role: Verbenia is devastated. She feels that her life has just begun—and now that it might be cut cruelly short. Verbenia knows she is worried and upset, but really doesn't want to talk about it. She views herself as a private person who doesn't feel comfortable sharing personal information, especially with strangers. Talking about her own breast, for heaven's sakes, is even worse.

Worker Role: You are a hospital social worker. Verbenia has been referred to you after her physician noted the presence of a breast lump during her annual exam. The procedure at this particular hospital's health clinic is to refer patients who are anxious about diagnoses to social workers for information and counseling.

Role-Play B: Silence and AIDS

Client Role: Hank has just learned that he is HIV positive. He had visited a confidential testing site two weeks ago and just got his results today. He has had numerous female sexual partners and figures that is how he contracted HIV. He's in such shock he can hardly talk.

Worker Role: You work at a crisis intervention unit. People with problems come in off of the street for help. Hank just walked into the unit and was referred to you.

---

[2] The supplementary material for Role-Plays A and B is taken from C. Zastrow and K. Kirst-Ashman, *Understanding Human Behavior and the Social Environment* (Chicago: Nelson-Hall, 4th ed., 1997). The supplementary material for Role C is taken from chapter 7 of the text which addresses dealing with grief.

C. The client for the chosen role play should take her or his place at the front of the class. Class members should then take turns asking questions. This can proceed for fifteen to twenty minutes.

D. The instructor will intervene and begin a class discussion.

E. Answer the following questions about the role-play:

1. Which techniques and responses demonstrated by class members appeared to be the most effective?

2. Which techniques and responses didn't seem to work? What do you think were the reasons they didn't work?

3. What did "social workers" find most difficult about this role play?

4.   What feelings and reactions did the client experience while doing the role play?

5.   How helpful was the information about breast cancer?

6   What did you learn from this role play?

Chapter 2 Competencies/Practice Behaviors Exercises Assessment:

Name: _____ Date: _____
Supervisor's Name: _____

Focus Competencies/Practice Behaviors:

- EP 2.1.1b   Practice personal reflection and self-correction to assure continual professional development
- EP 2.1.2a   Recognize and manage personal values in a way that allows professional values to guide practice
- EP 2.1.2c   Tolerate ambiguity in resolving ethical conflicts
- EP 2.1.10a   Substantively and affectively prepare for action with individuals, families, groups, organizations, and communities
- EP 2.1.10b   Use empathy and other interpersonal skills
- EP 2.1.10d   Collect, organize, and interpret client data

Instructions:

A.   Evaluate your work or your partner's work in the Focus Competencies/Practice Behaviors by completing the Competencies/Practice Behaviors Assessment form below

B.   What other Competencies/Practice Behaviors did you use to complete these Exercises? Be sure to record them in your assessments

1.	I have attained this competency/practice behavior (in the range of 81 to 100%)
2.	I have largely attained this competency/practice behavior (in the range of 61 to 80%)
3.	I have partially attained this competency/practice behavior (in the range of 41 to 60%)
4.	I have made a little progress in attaining this competency/practice behavior (in the range of 21 to 40%)
5.	I have made almost no progress in attaining this competency/practice behavior (in the range of 0 to 20%)

EPAS 2008 Core Competencies & Core Practice Behaviors							Student Self Assessment		Evaluator Feedback
Student and Evaluator Assessment Scale and Comments	0	1	2	3	4	5			**Agree/Disagree/Comments**
EP 2.1.1 Identify as a Professional Social Worker and Conduct Oneself Accordingly:									
a. Advocate for client access to the services of social work									
b. Practice personal reflection and self-correction to assure continual professional development									
c. Attend to professional roles and boundaries									
d. Demonstrate professional demeanor in behavior, appearance, and communication									
e. Engage in career-long learning									
f. Use supervision and consultation									
EP 2.1.2 Apply Social Work Ethical Principles to Guide Professional Practice:									
a. Recognize and manage personal values in a way that allows professional values to guide practice									
b. Make ethical decisions by applying NASW Code of Ethics and, as applicable, of the IFSW/IASSW Ethics in Social Work, Statement of Principles									
c. Tolerate ambiguity in resolving ethical conflicts									

d. Apply strategies of ethical reasoning to arrive at principled decisions						
EP 2.1.3 Apply Critical Thinking to Inform and Communicate Professional Judgments:						
a. Distinguish, appraise, and integrate multiple sources of knowledge, including research-based knowledge and practice wisdom						
b. Analyze models of assessment, prevention, intervention, and evaluation						
c. Demonstrate effective oral and written communication in working with individuals, families, groups, organizations, communities, and colleagues						
EP 2.1.4 Engage Diversity and Difference in Practice:						
a. Recognize the extent to which a culture's structures and values may oppress, marginalize, alienate, or create or enhance privilege and power						
b. Gain sufficient self-awareness to eliminate the influence of personal biases and values in working with diverse groups						
c. Recognize and communicate their understanding of the importance of difference in shaping life experiences						
d. View themselves as learners and engage those with whom they work as informants						
EP 2.1.5 Advance Human Rights and Social and Economic Justice:						
a. Understand forms and mechanisms of oppression and discrimination						
b. Advocate for human rights and social and economic justice						
c. Engage in practices that advance social and economic justice						
EP 2.1.6 Engage in Research-Informed Practice and Practice-Informed Research:						
a. Use practice experience to inform scientific inquiry						
b. Use research evidence to inform practice						
EP 2.1.7 Apply Knowledge of Human Behavior and the Social Environment:						
a. Utilize conceptual frameworks to guide the processes of assessment, intervention, and evaluation						
b. Critique and apply knowledge to understand person and environment						
EP 2.1.8 Engage in Policy Practice to Advance Social and Economic Well-Being and to Deliver Effective Social Work Services:						
a. Analyze, formulate, and advocate for policies that advance social well-being						
b. Collaborate with colleagues and clients for effective policy action						
EP 2.1.9 Respond to Contexts that Shape Practice:						
a. Continuously discover, appraise, and attend to changing locales, populations, scientific and technological developments, and emerging societal trends to provide relevant services						
b. Provide leadership in promoting sustainable changes in service delivery and practice to improve the quality of social services						

40

EP 2.1.10 Engage, Assess, Intervene, and Evaluate with Individuals, Families, Groups, Organizations and Communities:						
a. Substantively and affectively prepare for action with individuals, families, groups, organizations, and communities						
b. Use empathy and other interpersonal skills						
c. Develop a mutually agreed-on focus of work and desired outcomes						
d. Collect, organize, and interpret client data						
e. Assess client strengths and limitations						
f. Develop mutually agreed-on intervention goals and objectives						
g. Select appropriate intervention strategies						
h. Initiate actions to achieve organizational goals						
i. Implement prevention interventions that enhance client capacities						
j. Help clients resolve problems						
k. Negotiate, mediate, and advocate for clients						
l. Facilitate transitions and endings						
m. Critically analyze, monitor, and evaluate interventions						

Chapter 3
Mezzo Practice Skills: Working with Groups

Competencies/Practice Behaviors Exercise 3.1
Brainstorming

Focus Competencies or Practice Behaviors:
- EP 2.1.3   Apply critical thinking to inform and communicate professional judgments
- EP 2.1.5b   Advocate for human rights and social and economic justice
- EP 2.1.8   Engage in policy practice to advance social and economic well-being and to deliver effective social work services
- EP 2.1.10j Help clients resolve problems

Instructions:

A.   Help the group achieve its goal in the following vignette. This exercise can be done in class or out of class with friends.

> **Vignette**
> You are members of the "Respect Diversity" task force on your campus. The task force is responding to a series of physical and verbal attacks directed at gay and lesbian students. Your responsibility is to provide the college president with a list of ideas on how the school can encourage respect for diversity on your campus. She has said that the school has a substantial budget to pursue this project and wants your group to give her all the help you can.

B.   Assign one person to act as the group leader. That person will be responsible for ensuring that the group follows proper procedures. For example, this person will be responsible for ensuring that members do not stop to evaluate each idea and that all who wish to participate have an opportunity. Members should raise their hands before participating. The leader should encourage all contributions and clarify any ideas that are not clear. Additionally, the leader will write down the ideas generated by the group.

C.   Remember that the goal is to generate as many ideas as possible. No attempt is made to rate or evaluate the ideas. Members should be free to present ideas they thought of after hearing other members' contributions.

D.   The group leader begins by asking who wants to provide the first idea. She or he then writes the first idea on the board or flip chart.

E.   The group continues this process until all ideas have been collected.

F.   After the brainstorming has ended, answer the following questions and issues:

1.   What are the positive aspects of using such a brainstorming technique?

2.   What are the negative aspects?

3.   What specifically would the task group present to the college president?

4.   Summarize the specific steps used in this brainstorming process.

5.   What other situations can you envision where brainstorming might be harmful?

Competencies/Practice Behaviors Exercise 3.2
An Ice Breaker

Focus Competencies or Practice Behaviors:
- EP 2.1.3   Apply critical thinking to inform and communicate professional judgments

Instructions:
A.   Consider the fact that many people pursue a number of careers in their lives that are different from the one for which they were trained. Take a few minutes to jot down two careers other than social work in which you have some interest. Assume that you might be able to switch to any one of them at a later point in your life.
B.   Next to each career write down the characteristic you find most attractive about this career.
C.   Next, list a disadvantage or problem with that career.

43

Focus Competencies or Practice Behaviors:
- EP 2.1.10   Engage, assess, intervene, and evaluate with individuals, families, groups, organizations, and communities
- EP 2.1.10a Substantively and affectively prepare for action with individuals, families, groups, organizations, and communities

Instructions:
A.   Divide the class into groups of four to five.
B.   You will be asked to participate in the following exercise:

> **Exercise**
>   The social work program at your school must develop a retention policy that identifies the factors that would result in a student being counseled out of social work. The program is required to do this by its accreditation body, but faculty members want to have student input into the decision. As the student members of the program's advisory board, you have been asked to formulate at least five actions or behaviors which would warrant dismissal from social work.
>   Your fellow students have decided this is such an important activity that you must reach consensus on the five actions or behaviors. That is to say, you may not vote or otherwise decide based on majority opinion. Your input must reflect substantial agreement of all members.

C.   Try to follow these guidelines in order to reach consensus:
1.   To make decisions by consensus requires an atmosphere of openness where all members have an opportunity to be heard and to influence the ultimate outcome.
2.   Each member should be able to present ideas without being criticized.
3.   Opposing views should be solicited and creative solutions encouraged.
4.   The emphasis is on finding the best solution instead of on getting one's way.
D.   Select one member as both leader and recorder to help get the process underway. You might consider having each member contribute two ideas to the project, then rank-order each of the suggestions after discussing the merits and demerits of each.
E.   Report your results back to the larger group.
F.   The entire class can then pursue the following questions:

1.   How did your experience with consensus decision making compare with past decision-making activities in which you have been involved?

2.   What are some barriers to using a consensus model of decision making?

3.   What are the advantages to this method of making decisions?

Competencies/Practice Behaviors Exercise 3.4
Role-Play: Parliamentary Procedure

Focus Competencies or Practice Behaviors:
- EP 2.1.10   Engage, assess, intervene, and evaluate with individuals, families, groups, organizations, and communities

Instructions:
A.   This exercise is designed to familiarize you with the terminology and procedure used in groups operating under *Robert's Rules of Order*. The example given is of a social work student organization. Various roles are identified. Those playing the roles read the appropriate portions of the transcript.

B.   The instructor will assign specific roles to individual students (there are a total of eleven roles, plus those of members-at-large). Members-at-large will vote on all issues before the group.

C.   The roles are: president, vice president, treasurer, secretary, chair of the activities committee, chair of the faculty relations committee, chair of the social action committee, and members 1, 2, 3, and 4.

D.   Each person playing a role will read his or her script from the transcript of the meeting. It is important to stay alert and recognize your part.

E.   Feel free at any point to ask the instructor about the purpose or meaning of any particular motion.

F.   At the end of the role play, answer the following questions:

45

1. Why is there such a seemingly rigid set of steps to be followed in parliamentary procedure (such as making a motion, seconding it, debating, and voting on it)?

2. What steps in this process appear most confusing to you?

3. Why does Robert's Rules of Order prevent a person who voted with the losing side from asking to have the matter reconsidered later?

Parliamentary Procedure Role Play
The Social Work Student Organization

President: The meeting of the Social Work Student Organization is called to order. The minutes of the April 1st meeting have been distributed. Is there a motion for approval?

Vice President: I move approval of the minutes of the April 1st meeting.

President: Is there a second?

Chair of Social Action Committee: I second the motion.

President: Is there any discussion?

Chair of Faculty Relations Committee: I think my motion last time was to ask the faculty to provide three spots on the advisory board for student representatives, not four as the minutes show.

Secretary: I think she's right. That appears to be a typo. It should have been three, not four.

President: Are there any more changes? If not, I'll ask for a vote to approve the minutes. All in favor of approving the minutes with the change noted, please say Aye.

All: Aye.

President: All opposed, please say no. The motion passes.

President: May we have the Treasurer's report, please.

Treasurer: My report has also been distributed. It shows a balance of $240.04 after our car smash fund-raiser. We only had one bill and that was dry cleaning to get the oil out of Professor Mower's sports coat from the car smash. He's such a good sport, he didn't even complain about the rest of his clothes. Are there any questions about the Treasurer's report?

President: A motion to accept the Treasurer's report is in order.

Member 1: I move to accept the Treasurer's report.

Member 2: I second the motion.

President: All in favor of the motion, please say Aye.

All: Aye.

President: All opposed?

President: The motion passes unanimously.

President: Does the Activity Committee have a report?

Chair of Activities Committee: Thank you. Yes, we do. The committee has organized the second Urban Plunge trip for the 29th of the month. We will be visiting Metropolis and spending the weekend in a homeless shelter. We will be leaving campus Friday at noon, working in the shelter Saturday and Sunday, and returning to campus Monday morning. We have room for two more people in the van. The cost is $25 plus a share of the gas. This looks like a good opportunity to learn more about the homeless first hand, and to talk to social workers from other agencies. Any questions?

Secretary: I'd like to move that our organization pay for the gas costs since we are sponsoring this activity.

President: It has been moved that SWSO pay for the gas for this trip. Is there a second?
Member 1: I second the motion.

President: Any discussion

Treasurer: I'd like to amend the motion to set a limit of $50 on the gas costs.

47

President: Is there a second? I don't hear a second so the amendment dies. Is there any further discussion on the original motion? Hearing none, all in favor of the motion, please say Aye.

All but Treasurer: Aye.

President: All opposed, say no.

Treasurer: No.

President: The motion carries. The Activities Committee will let the Treasurer know what the gas costs and he will reimburse you.

President: I believe the Social Action Committee has a report.

Chair of Social Action Committee: Yes, we do. We are in the final stages of planning for our social action day. At present, we have a speaker from the Gay and Lesbian Organization speaking on the latest campus problems faced by their members; another speaker from the Action Coalition, who will talk about how student organizations can join together to bring about social change; and a representative from the Chippewa Tribe, who will speak on tribal rights and history.

We have also planned a letter-writing to get the local paper and media to focus their attention on the *Cinco de Mayo* Chicano festival. We're working with the Chicano Student Organization on this project. Are there any questions?

President: Thanks for your report.

President: Is there any other old business?

Vice President: I move we disband the Social Action Committee. They're getting too radical for me.

President: You're out of order, Orrin, we already discussed and voted on that matter last time.

Vice President: I move to reconsider our previous decision. *Chair of Activities Committee:* Point of order.

President: What is your point of order?

Chair of Activities Committee: Orrin voted with the losing side on that previous vote. He is not permitted to move for reconsideration. Only a person who voted on the winning side can make such a motion.

President: You are correct. Again, Orrin, your motion is out of order. Is there any new business?

Member 2: I move that we hold an end-of-year party, like last year.

Member 1: I second the motion.

President: It's been moved and seconded to have an end-of-year party. Is there discussion?

Member 3: Given the time of day, I move we refer this motion to the Activities Committee and ask them to report by our next meeting.

Member 4: I second the motion.

President: All in favor of referring the party idea to the Activities Committee say Aye.

All: Aye.

President: All opposed, say no.

President: The Ayes have it. This matter is referred to the Activities Committee. If there is no other business to come before us, I declare the meeting adjourned.

Chapter 3 Competencies/Practice Behaviors Exercises Assessment:

Name: _____ **Date:** _____

Supervisor's Name: _____

Focus Competencies/Practice Behaviors:
- EP 2.1.3   Apply critical thinking to inform and communicate professional judgments
- EP 2.1.5b   Advocate for human rights and social and economic justice
- EP 2.1.8   Engage in policy practice to advance social and economic well-being and to deliver effective social work services
- EP 2.1.10   Engage, assess, intervene, and evaluate with individuals, families, groups, organizations and communities
- EP 2.1.10a Substantively and affectively prepare for action with individuals, families, groups, organizations, and communities
- EP 2.1.10j Help clients resolve problems

Instructions:

A.   Evaluate your work or your partner's work in the Focus Competencies/Practice Behaviors by completing the Competencies/Practice Behaviors Assessment form below

B.   What other Competencies/Practice Behaviors did you use to complete these Exercises? Be sure to record them in your assessments

1.	I have attained this competency/practice behavior (in the range of 81 to 100%)
2.	I have largely attained this competency/practice behavior (in the range of 61 to 80%)
3.	I have partially attained this competency/practice behavior (in the range of 41 to 60%)
4.	I have made a little progress in attaining this competency/practice behavior (in the range of 21 to 40%)
5.	I have made almost no progress in attaining this competency/practice behavior (in the range of 0 to 20%)

EPAS 2008 Core Competencies & Core Practice Behaviors	Student Self Assessment						Evaluator Feedback
Student and Evaluator Assessment Scale and Comments	0	1	2	3	4	5	Agree/Disagree/Comments
EP 2.1.1 Identify as a Professional Social Worker and Conduct Oneself Accordingly:							
a. Advocate for client access to the services of social work							
b. Practice personal reflection and self-correction to assure continual professional development							
c. Attend to professional roles and boundaries							
d. Demonstrate professional demeanor in behavior, appearance, and communication							
e. Engage in career-long learning							
f. Use supervision and consultation							
EP 2.1.2 Apply Social Work Ethical Principles to Guide Professional Practice:							
a. Recognize and manage personal values in a way that allows professional values to guide practice							
b. Make ethical decisions by applying NASW Code of Ethics and, as applicable, of the IFSW/IASSW Ethics in Social Work, Statement of Principles							

50

c. Tolerate ambiguity in resolving ethical conflicts						
d. Apply strategies of ethical reasoning to arrive at principled decisions						
EP 2.1.3 Apply Critical Thinking to Inform and Communicate Professional Judgments:						
a. Distinguish, appraise, and integrate multiple sources of knowledge, including research-based knowledge and practice wisdom						
b. Analyze models of assessment, prevention, intervention, and evaluation						
c. Demonstrate effective oral and written communication in working with individuals, families, groups, organizations, communities, and colleagues						
EP 2.1.4 Engage Diversity and Difference in Practice:						
a. Recognize the extent to which a culture's structures and values may oppress, marginalize, alienate, or create or enhance privilege and power						
b. Gain sufficient self-awareness to eliminate the influence of personal biases and values in working with diverse groups						
c. Recognize and communicate their understanding of the importance of difference in shaping life experiences						
d. View themselves as learners and engage those with whom they work as informants						
EP 2.1.5 Advance Human Rights and Social and Economic Justice:						
a. Understand forms and mechanisms of oppression and discrimination						
b. Advocate for human rights and social and economic justice						
c. Engage in practices that advance social and economic justice						
EP 2.1.6 Engage in Research-Informed Practice and Practice-Informed Research:						
a. Use practice experience to inform scientific inquiry						
b. Use research evidence to inform practice						
EP 2.1.7 Apply Knowledge of Human Behavior and the Social Environment:						
a. Utilize conceptual frameworks to guide the processes of assessment, intervention, and evaluation						
b. Critique and apply knowledge to understand person and environment						
EP 2.1.8 Engage in Policy Practice to Advance Social and Economic Well-Being and to Deliver Effective Social Work Services:						
a. Analyze, formulate, and advocate for policies that advance social well-being						
b. Collaborate with colleagues and clients for effective policy action						
EP 2.1.9 Respond to Contexts that Shape Practice:						
a. Continuously discover, appraise, and attend to changing locales, populations, scientific and technological developments, and emerging societal trends to provide relevant services						

51

b.	Provide leadership in promoting sustainable changes in service delivery and practice to improve the quality of social services						
EP 2.1.10 Engage, Assess, Intervene, and Evaluate with Individuals, Families, Groups, Organizations and Communities:							
a.	Substantively and affectively prepare for action with individuals, families, groups, organizations, and communities						
b.	Use empathy and other interpersonal skills						
c.	Develop a mutually agreed-on focus of work and desired outcomes						
d.	Collect, organize, and interpret client data						
e.	Assess client strengths and limitations						
f.	Develop mutually agreed-on intervention goals and objectives						
g.	Select appropriate intervention strategies						
h.	Initiate actions to achieve organizational goals						
i.	Implement prevention interventions that enhance client capacities						
j.	Help clients resolve problems						
k.	Negotiate, mediate, and advocate for clients						
l.	Facilitate transitions and endings						
m.	Critically analyze, monitor, and evaluate interventions						

Competencies/Practice Behaviors Exercise 4.1
Preparing a Press Release

Focus Competencies or Practice Behaviors:
- EP 2.1.1d   Demonstrate professional demeanor in behavior, appearance, and communication
- EP 2.1.3c   Demonstrate effective oral and written communication in working with individuals, families, groups, organizations, communities, and colleagues

Instructions:
A.   There are a number of reasons why you might write a news release for your agency. These include announcement of a new service provided by the agency, the need to publicize an existing program, or a desire to recruit volunteers or foster parents. Working with and using the news media to publicize events, activities, and perspectives is an essential skill. News releases are one of the easiest and simplest ways to keep the media informed about your agency or activity. As in any news article, basic information is expected by the reader. This includes such items as who, what, where, why, when, and how.

B.   Read the following example of an agency news release. It was written to publicize the creation of a new program and provides information about services provided, hours of operation, and contact persons.

Rural Mental Health Clinic
12 East North Street
East North Overshoe, Vermont
802/658-0371

For Immediate Release:

Drug and Alcohol Program a First in State

EAST NORTH OVERSHOE, VT—December 28, 2004, The Rural Mental Health Clinic has added a drug and alcohol program to its new service center in East North Overshoe.

According to the Director, Jim Beam, the new program is the first in the state to offer both inpatient and outpatient service to chemically addicted individuals. The clinic has added three staff members and will be hosting an open house on Friday, January 14, from 1:00-3:00 p.m. The office for the new program is at 232 Spring Street.

For further information, contact Jim Beam at 658-0371 or 658-9981.

C.   Now prepare your own news release. Put yourself in the following role:

> **Scenario**
> You are the director of a new agency established to coordinate services to families in Clearwater City. Your agency was set up through the cooperative efforts of four existing agencies which felt they could better serve families in need by pooling their resources. You want the community to know about your agency and about the fact that several agencies acted cooperatively to launch this program. You also want them to know that taxpayers' money is being used in a positive fashion.
>
> There is only one newspaper in your city, the *Daily Planet*, and no other print media. There is a radio station that plays funeral dirges all day and does not have any news programs. Their only public service announcements cover the openings of new mortuaries and the daily obituaries. Plan your news release to convey information succinctly and in an interesting manner.

D.   In the release, remember to include the following elements:
   a.   *Who* (person or agency) is this news release about?
   b.   *What* is important enough to deserve a news article?
   c.   *When* did or will this event occur?
   d.   *Where* or in what location did this event occur?
   e.   *Why* is this being brought to the attention of the public?
   f.   *How* did this event occur?

The entire release should be no longer than one page. Take about 20 minutes to write it. Remember that, although this release will be handwritten for the purposes of this assignment, a real release would be typewritten, double-spaced, with margins of at least 1 ½ inches on each side of the page.

E.   After you complete your release, answer the following questions:

1.   What are the similarities among the various releases?

2.   What are the differences?

3.   What did you find most difficult about writing the release?

4.   Describe in your own words how such a news release might benefit the agency for which you work.

Competencies/Practice Behaviors Exercise 4.2
Letter Writing

Focus Competencies or Practice Behaviors:
- EP 2.1.1d   Demonstrate professional demeanor in behavior, appearance, and communication
- EP 2.1.3c   Demonstrate effective oral and written communication in working with individuals, families, groups, organizations, communities, and colleagues

Instructions:

A.   Review the instructions for writing a letter shown below. They are taken from Highlight 4.7 in the text.

Letter Writing Strategies
To be effective, letters:
a.   Are planned carefully, revised, polished, and proofread;
b.   Include letterhead (with address), date, salutation (Dear ___), body, complimentary close (Sincerely), and both typed and written signature;
c.   Are businesslike and pleasant;
d.   Are brief (preferably one page) and discuss only one topic;
e.   Open with a positive comment;
f.   Are factual, and simply written;
g.   Should have perfect grammar and spelling; and
h.   Request a response.

    Letters which are less likely to be effective include those that appear identical, those copied out of newspaper advertisements, or clearly mass-produced letters (e.g., duplicated copies instead of original). Letters which attack the reader are less likely to work and may backfire. Some people advocate handwritten letters, but the advantages of a clear, typed message outweigh the advantages of a handwritten communication.

    If letters are to be mass-produced, as might be desired when a group is trying to sway the reader, at least vary the letters so that they don't appear identical. Written letters are helpful in certain situations and help create a record of communication with the decision-maker. They should be used as an adjunct to, and not instead of, other more personal forms of contact. Person-to-person communication is still superior to written messages as a means of influencing other people.

B.　　　Now read the business letter shown below. In a number of ways, it is very poorly constructed.

> January 31, 2005
>
> Mr. Raul Prenner
> Department of Aging
> 1492 Columbus Way
> Santa Maria, NY 00923
>
> Dear Mr. Prenner:
>
> 　　　You've got your nerve telling my client she isn't eligible for your program. I don't know how you get off with your attitude. It's really poor. My client and I think you need to change your policy so that people like my client can use your agency.
> 　　　I think we need to get together to talk about your silly policies at my earliest convenience. Please call my office and arrange for an appointment immediately.
>
> Yours Truly,
>
> Edgar J. Hoover
> Social Worker

C.　　　List the things that are wrong with this letter. This may include the tone of the letter and the absence of important information.

D.　　　Now on a separate sheet of paper, rewrite this letter using the same general information contained in the poorly written letter. This time, use your own name and address. Be careful to conform to the standards for effectiveness described.

E.　　　After completing the letters, the entire class can discuss the results. Answer the following questions.

　　　1.　　　In what specific ways was the original letter poorly written?

　　　2.　　　In what specific ways could the original letter be improved?

3.   What things were the most difficult about writing your own letter?

4.   What might be some of the reasons for writing letters in social work practice?

Competencies/Practice Behaviors Exercise 4.3
Connecting Roles and Responsibilities

Focus Competencies or Practice Behaviors:
- EP 2.1.1   Identify as a professional social worker and conduct oneself accordingly
- EP 2.1.1c   Attend to professional roles and boundaries
- EP 2.1.3   Apply critical thinking to inform and communicate professional judgments

Instructions:
A.   Review the two columns shown below. In one column are the role titles frequently associated with change efforts in communities and organizations. In the second column are descriptions of various roles.

Role Titles	Role Descriptions
A. Initiator	1. Decides what the client is entitled to and what is keeping the client from receiving what she needs. Requires worker to assess an adversary's strengths and weaknesses.
B. Negotiator	2. Represents an organization or group trying to gain something from another group. Seeks win-win situations and a middle ground that both sides can accept.
C. Advocate	3. Calls attention to an issue such as a problem existing in the community, an unmet need, or a situation to be improved.

57

D. Spokesperson	4. Helps two sides work out a compromise. The role player is neutral, not siding with either party. One task involves ensuring that both sides understand the other's positions.
E. Organizer	5. Provides advice, suggestions, or ideas to another person, group, or organization. Two characteristics are important: knowing more than the person being helped; and the ability to see her advice ignored without getting personally involved or hurt.
F. Mediator	6. Presents an organization's views to others without coloring them with his or her own opinions.
G. Consultant	7. Creates groups of people who share a similar concern. Tasks include developing the leadership potential of others, stimulating others to act, and identifying targets for change.

B.   Match the role titles with the role descriptions.

C.   Review this information in the text. Compare your answers with the correct ones.

D.   Answer the following questions:

1.   What roles were the most difficult for you to understand?

2.   Describe possible agency situations where each role might be used.

3. What are examples of practice situations in which workers might assume more than one role?

4. Are there situations in which workers might have to assume roles that conflict with each other? If so, how might these roles conflict?

Competencies/Practice Behaviors Exercise 4.4
Role-Play: Professional Roles in Organizational and Community Change

Focus Competencies or Practice Behaviors:
- EP 2.1.1a   Advocate for client access to the services of social work
- EP 2.1.1c   Attend to professional roles and boundaries
- EP 2.1.1d   Demonstrate professional demeanor in behavior, appearance, and communication
- EP 2.1.1f   Use supervision and consultation
- EP 2.1.3c   Demonstrate effective oral and written communication in working with individuals, families, groups, organizations, communities, and colleagues
- EP 2.1.5b   Advocate for human rights and social and economic justice
- EP 2.1.8b   Collaborate with colleagues and clients for effective policy action
- EP 2.1.9b   Provide leadership in promoting sustainable changes in service delivery and practice to improve the quality of social services
- EP 2.1.10k   Negotiate, mediate, and advocate for clients

Instructions:
A. Thinking of a practitioner's work as a series of roles is possible and sometimes helpful. Using some of the roles described in the text, assign a separate role for each person in the role-play.
B. The scenario begins in the boardroom of the Haversham County Department of Human Services. It is budget time and some programs are going to "get the axe." Everyone is here to save their programs from being cut or downsized, and therefore, their own positions as well.

59

The **mediator, Serenity,** is from the Mayor's office in Bixbee, which is the largest city in Haversham County. Serenity is here to help resolve disagreements among the various participants, and help take the emotion out of the situation, allowing better problem solving.

The **consultant, Constance,** has been brought in to advise on zoning laws and to help groups become more effective. Constance has been a constant member of these types of meetings and is able to see whatever advice she gives ignored without becoming offended. If a consultee chooses to ignore Constance's advice, no matter how good, then she accepts that the person has this right.

Oranthal, the **organizer**, is the one who coordinates individuals in the group. He believes that if all of the agencies and workers come together in an organized manner, improvements can result.

Angie is the **advocate** in this meeting. She is very capable of using pressure tactics to achieve the most for the clients being served in her department, which is the child protective services area. Angie believes her department is woefully understaffed and that burnout is prevalent throughout—much more so than any other department represented here.

The **initiator, Ivan**, sees that the agency's office hours are forcing clients to come at difficult times, resulting in lost pay and jeopardizing their jobs. He has been working on a plan where the agency uses flextime, thereby balancing the worker's own preferences with the needs of the clients who cannot get to the agency during a typical 9-to-5 schedule.

C. Begin the role-play and continue for about 20 minutes. Each of you stay in character and see if you can actually come to an agreement. After the 20 minutes, discuss the difficulties you encountered.

D. Answer the following questions:

1. What type of meeting protocol was established? Did you use something formal like *Robert's Rules of Order*, or was it more informal? Do you think some other meeting protocol should have been used? If so, what and why?

2. What were some of the barriers to the decision making?

3.   What thoughts and ideas did you gain from this exercise about vying for limited resources?

4.   What feelings and reactions did you experience while doing the role play?

Chapter 4 Competencies/Practice Behaviors Exercises Assessment:

Name: _____ **Date:** _____

Supervisor's Name: _____

Focus Competencies/Practice Behaviors:

- EP 2.1.1   Identify as a professional social worker and conduct oneself accordingly
- EP 2.1.1a   Advocate for client access to the services of social work
- EP 2.1.1c   Attend to professional roles and boundaries
- EP 2.1.1d   Demonstrate professional demeanor in behavior, appearance, and communication
- EP 2.1.1f   Use supervision and consultation
- EP 2.1.3   Apply critical thinking to inform and communicate professional judgments
- EP 2.1.3c   Demonstrate effective oral and written communication in working with individuals, families, groups, organizations, communities, and colleagues
- EP 2.1.5b   Advocate for human rights and social and economic justice
- EP 2.1.8b   Collaborate with colleagues and clients for effective policy action
- EP 2.1.9b   Provide leadership in promoting sustainable changes in service delivery and practice to improve the quality of social services
- EP 2.1.10a   Substantively and affectively prepare for action with individuals, families, groups, organizations, and communities
- EP 2.1.10b   Use empathy and other interpersonal skills
- EP 2.1.10c   Develop a mutually agreed-on focus of work and desired outcomes
- EP 2.1.10d   Collect, organize, and interpret client data
- EP 2.1.10e   Assess client strengths and limitations
- EP 2.1.10f   Develop mutually agreed-on intervention goals and objectives
- EP 2.1.10g   Select appropriate intervention strategies
- EP 2.1.10j   Help clients resolve problems
- EP 2.1.10k   Negotiate, mediate, and advocate for clients

Instructions:

A.   Evaluate your work or your partner's work in the Focus Competencies/Practice Behaviors by completing the Competencies/Practice Behaviors Assessment form below

B.   What other Competencies/Practice Behaviors did you use to complete these Exercises? Be sure to record them in your assessments

1.	I have attained this competency/practice behavior (in the range of 81 to 100%)
2.	I have largely attained this competency/practice behavior (in the range of 61 to 80%)
3.	I have partially attained this competency/practice behavior (in the range of 41 to 60%)
4.	I have made a little progress in attaining this competency/practice behavior (in the range of 21 to 40%)
5.	I have made almost no progress in attaining this competency/practice behavior (in the range of 0 to 20%)

EPAS 2008 Core Competencies & Core Practice Behaviors	Student Self Assessment						Evaluator Feedback
Student and Evaluator Assessment Scale and Comments	0	1	2	3	4	5	**Agree/Disagree/Comments**
EP 2.1.1 Identify as a Professional Social Worker and Conduct Oneself Accordingly:							
a. Advocate for client access to the services of social work							
b. Practice personal reflection and self-correction to assure continual professional development							
c. Attend to professional roles and boundaries							
d. Demonstrate professional demeanor in behavior, appearance, and communication							
e. Engage in career-long learning							
f. Use supervision and consultation							
EP 2.1.2 Apply Social Work Ethical Principles to Guide Professional Practice:							
a. Recognize and manage personal values in a way that allows professional values to guide practice							
b. Make ethical decisions by applying NASW Code of Ethics and, as applicable, of the IFSW/IASSW Ethics in Social Work, Statement of Principles							
c. Tolerate ambiguity in resolving ethical conflicts							
d. Apply strategies of ethical reasoning to arrive at principled decisions							
EP 2.1.3 Apply Critical Thinking to Inform and Communicate Professional Judgments:							
a. Distinguish, appraise, and integrate multiple sources of knowledge, including research-based knowledge and practice wisdom							
b. Analyze models of assessment, prevention, intervention, and evaluation							
c. Demonstrate effective oral and written communication in working with individuals, families, groups, organizations, communities, and colleagues							
EP 2.1.4 Engage Diversity and Difference in Practice:							
a. Recognize the extent to which a culture's structures and values may oppress, marginalize, alienate, or create or enhance privilege and power							
b. Gain sufficient self-awareness to eliminate the influence of personal biases and values in working with diverse groups							
c. Recognize and communicate their understanding of the importance of difference in shaping life experiences							
d. View themselves as learners and engage those with whom they work as informants							
EP 2.1.5 Advance Human Rights and Social and Economic Justice:							
a. Understand forms and mechanisms of oppression and discrimination							
b. Advocate for human rights and social and economic justice							

63

c.	Engage in practices that advance social and economic justice						
EP 2.1.6 Engage in Research-Informed Practice and Practice-Informed Research:							
a.	Use practice experience to inform scientific inquiry						
b.	Use research evidence to inform practice						
EP 2.1.7 Apply Knowledge of Human Behavior and the Social Environment:							
a.	Utilize conceptual frameworks to guide the processes of assessment, intervention, and evaluation						
b.	Critique and apply knowledge to understand person and environment						
EP 2.1.8 Engage in Policy Practice to Advance Social and Economic Well-Being and to Deliver Effective Social Work Services:							
a.	Analyze, formulate, and advocate for policies that advance social well-being						
b.	Collaborate with colleagues and clients for effective policy action						
EP 2.1.9 Respond to Contexts that Shape Practice:							
a.	Continuously discover, appraise, and attend to changing locales, populations, scientific and technological developments, and emerging societal trends to provide relevant services						
b.	Provide leadership in promoting sustainable changes in service delivery and practice to improve the quality of social services						
EP 2.1.10 Engage, Assess, Intervene, and Evaluate with Individuals, Families, Groups, Organizations and Communities:							
a.	Substantively and affectively prepare for action with individuals, families, groups, organizations, and communities						
b.	Use empathy and other interpersonal skills						
c.	Develop a mutually agreed-on focus of work and desired outcomes						
d.	Collect, organize, and interpret client data						
e.	Assess client strengths and limitations						
f.	Develop mutually agreed-on intervention goals and objectives						
g.	Select appropriate intervention strategies						
h.	Initiate actions to achieve organizational goals						
i.	Implement prevention interventions that enhance client capacities						
j.	Help clients resolve problems						
k.	Negotiate, mediate, and advocate for clients						
l.	Facilitate transitions and endings						
m.	Critically analyze, monitor, and evaluate interventions						

64

Competencies/Practice Behaviors Exercise 5.1
Engagement

Focus Competencies or Practice Behaviors:
- EP 2.1.3   Apply critical thinking to inform and communicate professional judgments
- EP 2.1.10   Engage, assess, intervene, and evaluate with individuals, families, groups, organizations, and communities
- EP 2.1.10d   Collect, organize, and interpret client data

Instructions:
A.   Read the brief vignette below.

Vignette

   "Hi, Mary. I'm Derrick, your social worker here at the homeless shelter. I bet you really could use a shower and a meal." With those opening statements, Derrick Broder greeted Mary Livingston, a woman who had just sought shelter for herself and her child.

   "As you probably know, we don't charge too much here and you'll be glad you came to the shelter. We help lots of people with your problems."

   "Well, I don't know," said Mary. "I don't have much money."

   "Don't worry about a thing, Mary. Now lets get you and your little boy a bed and a meal. In the morning, I'll have my colleague, Monica, meet with you to discuss ways you can improve your child-rearing skills, too. You'll like her."

---

1.   Identify at least five errors or problems on the part of the worker.

2.   Explain what the worker should have done to conduct an effective engagement.

Focus Competencies or Practice Behaviors:
- EP 2.1.1e   Engage in career-long learning

Instructions:

A.   Before beginning the exercise, review the material in the text on assessment instruments.

B.   Take the Rathus Assertiveness Schedule (RAS) printed below.[1]

The Rathus Assertiveness Schedule (RAS)

Directions: Indicate how characteristic or descriptive each of the following statements is of you by using the code given below.

+3	Very characteristic of me, extremely descriptive
+2	Rather characteristic of me, quite descriptive
+1	Somewhat characteristic of me, slightly descriptive
-1	Somewhat uncharacteristic of me, slightly nondescriptive
-2	Rather uncharacteristic of me, quite nondescriptive
-3	Very uncharacteristic of me, extremely nondescriptive

_____   1.   Most people seem to be more aggressive and assertive than I am.

_____   2.   I have hesitated to make or accept dates because of shyness.

_____   3.   When the food served at a restaurant is not done to my satisfaction, I complain about it to the waiter or waitress.

_____   4.   I am careful to avoid hurting other people's feelings, even when I feel that I have been injured.

_____   5.   If a salesman has gone to considerable trouble to show me merchandise which is not quite suitable, I have a difficult time in saying "no."

_____   6.   When I am asked to do something, I insist upon knowing why.

_____   7.   There are times when I look for a good and vigorous argument.

_____   8.   I strive to get ahead as well as most people in my position.

_____   9.   To be honest, people often take advantage of me.

_____   10.   I enjoy starting conversations with new acquaintances and strangers.

_____   11.   I often don't know what to say to attractive persons of the opposite sex.

_____   12.   I will hesitate to make phone calls to business establishments and institutions.

_____   13.   I would rather apply for a job or for admission to a college by writing letters than by going through with personal interviews.

_____   14.   I find it embarrassing to return merchandise.

_____   15.   If a close and respected relative were annoying me, I would smother my feelings rather than express my annoyance.

_____   16.   I have avoided asking questions for fear of sounding stupid.

_____   17.   During an argument I am sometimes afraid that I will get so upset that I will shake all over.

---

[1] The Rathus Assertiveness Schedule and the accompanying scoring explanation are adapted from "Rathus Assertiveness Schedule: Normative and Factor-Analytic Data," by D.B. Hull and J.H. Hull, *Behavior Therapy*, 9 (September, 1978), p. 673. Reprinted with permission of the authors and the Association for the Advancement of Behavior Therapy, 15 W. 36th St., New York, NY 10018.

_____	18.	If a famed and respected lecturer makes a statement which I think is incorrect, I will have the audience hear my point of view as well.
_____	19.	I avoid arguing over prices with clerks and salesmen.
_____	20.	When I have done something important or worthwhile, I manage to let others know about it.
_____	21.	I am open and frank about my feelings.
_____	22.	If someone has been spreading false and bad stories about me, I see him (her) as soon as possible to "have a talk" about it.
_____	23.	I often have a hard time saying "no."
_____	24.	I tend to bottle up my emotions rather than make a scene.
_____	25.	I complain about poor service in a restaurant and elsewhere.
_____	26.	When I am given a complaint, I sometimes just don't know what to say.
_____	27.	If a couple near me in a theater or at a lecture were conversing rather loudly, I would ask them to be quiet or to take their conversation elsewhere.
_____	28.	Anyone attempting to push ahead of me in a line is in for a good battle.
_____	29.	I am quick to express an opinion.
_____	30.	There are times when I just can't say anything.

C. Score the RAS by following these procedures:

a.	Change the sign from positive (+) to negative (–) or from negative (–) to positive (+) for your answers to the following questions: 2, 4, 5, 9, 11, 12, 13, 14, 15, 16, 17, 19, 23, 24, 26, 30.
b.	Add up your total.

1) Scores of –90 to –20 means you're generally unassertive, and probably too much so. The lower your score, the less assertive you are.

2) Scores of –20 to +60 indicate you're within the realm of being appropriately assertive much of the time.

3) Scores of +60 to +90 mean you're very assertive or possibly aggressive. This is a warning category.

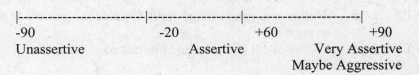

```
|--------------------------|------------------|-----------------------|
-90                       -20               +60                    +90
Unassertive                     Assertive           Very Assertive
                                                    Maybe Aggressive
```

D. Answer the following questions:

1. How assertive does the RAS indicate you are?

2. Do you think the RAS is accurate?

3. What did you learn about assertiveness and assertive behavior by taking the RAS?

4. What did you learn about improving assertiveness and assertive behavior by taking the RAS?

5. For what types of client problems and needs might the RAS be used in practice?

| **Competencies/Practice Behaviors Exercise 5.3** |
| **Genogram** |

Focus Competencies or Practice Behaviors:
- EP 2.1.7a   Utilize conceptual frameworks to guide the process of assessment, intervention, and evaluation
- EP 2.1.10e   Assess client strengths and limitations
-

Instructions:
A. Review the description and examples of a genogram contained in the text. Interview family members and other data sources to gather the information you require. Construct a genogram of your family.

1.   What can you conclude from your review of this genogram?

Competencies/Practice Behaviors Exercise 5.4
Role-Play: The Assessment Process

Focus Competencies or Practice Behaviors:
- EP 2.1.1c   Attend to professional roles and boundaries
- EP 2.1.10e   Assess client strengths and limitations
-

Instructions:

A.   Before beginning the exercise, review the material in the text on how to approach assessment, and on assessment from a micro practice perspective. A copy of the figure entitled "Assessment in the Generalist Intervention Model" is provided below. Follow these steps in your role play.

ASSESSMENT IN THE GENERALIST INTERVENTION MODEL

FOUNDATION FOR GENERALIST PRACTICE

KNOWLEDGE:
Fields of Practice
Practice Skills
HBSE
Research
Policy

SKILLS:
Common Generalist
Micro
Mezzo
Macro

VALUES
Professional Ethics
Identification of
Personal Values

↓

(ENGAGEMENT)

↓

ASSESSMENT

(STEP 1:) Identify your client.

↓

(STEP 2:) → (STEP 3:) → (STEP 4:)

Assess the client-
in-situation from
the following per-
spectives:

Cite information
about client
problems and
needs.

Identify client
strengths.

MICRO:	►	►
MEZZO:	►	►
MACRO:	►	►
ASPECTS OF DIVERSITY:	►	►

B. Divide up into pairs. One student in each pair will role play the client and the other the worker. The worker's task is to do an assessment of an elderly client as described below. The worker's job is intake worker for Horseradish County Social Services Department.

THE CLIENT

A concerned neighbor referred Grafton, seventy-seven, to the Horseradish County Elderly Protective Services Unit. Grafton lives on his rundown family farm on the outskirts of the rural Midwestern county. The neighbor reported that twice he found Grafton had fallen while walking out to get his mail, and the elderly man lay helplessly on the ground. Both times the neighbor had to practically carry Grafton back into the house. Grafton has rheumatoid arthritis, which makes it very difficult to walk even with his two canes. Additionally, his eyesight is very poor. The neighbor also raised questions about Grafton's ability to shop and cook for himself.

 Grafton's wife, Vicki, died two years ago after a long bout with intestinal cancer. Since her death, Grafton has remained isolated and alone. He has three sons. Only his oldest son, Ralph, forty-eight, lives nearby in a small town in Horseradish County. He owns a small pea canning factory. Ralph works long hours to keep his business afloat and has little time to spend with his own family, let alone with Grafton. Ralph and his second wife, Janet, have three teenage children.

 Grafton's second son, Chuck, forty-two, is a pop artist in San Francisco. The youngest, Jim, thirty-five, is a worm farmer in Idaho. Both are single.

 Grafton considers himself an intelligent, independent man who worked hard all of his life to make his farm successful. However, since his arthritis took a turn for the worse ten years ago, he has had to stop actively farming. He is now facing financial difficulties. He's experienced many years of little income and high health costs for both himself and his wife. He is becoming increasingly depressed at his failing health. However, he clings doggedly to the notion that he must remain on his farm. To do otherwise, he thinks to himself, would mean giving up and accepting certain death. Grafton is aware of the Happy Hunting Ground Health Care Center, the only nursing home in the area. He has sadly watched some of his friends enter it, and dreads the thought of having to do so himself.

 In summary, Grafton's problems include: failing health involving arthritis, poor eyesight, and intestinal distress (the last of which he does *not* like to talk about); loneliness; having few activities to keep him busy; and feeling unwanted and unimportant. Strengths include: intelligence; independence; ownership of the farm; having concerned children; and an outgoing, sociable personality. Some of Grafton's likes include: a love of reading classical novels (on bright days when his eyesight improves slightly); seeing his children; playing stud poker; and drinking beer.

C. The worker should follow the assessment process as described in the text. Notes should be taken as if the worker would have to write up an actual assessment report. The role-played interview should last from fifteen to twenty minutes. The worker may choose to focus on the following:

  a. Acknowledgement of the specific problems and issues involved.
  b. Identification of the actual pros and cons of remaining in his own home versus entering a nursing home.
  c. Emphasis on Grafton's strengths and how he might best put them to use.
  d. Micro, mezzo, and macro aspects of the situation and how they might be involved.
  e. Aspects of diversity which might be important.

71

The worker might choose to ask questions resembling the following:

a. "What do you plan to do regarding your health problems?"
b. "What do you feel you need at this time?"
c. "Would you be interested in trying . . . ?"
d. "How could you structure your time so that you'd be more able to do what you want to?" (See the figure in the text for additional questions to ask during assessment.)

The person playing Grafton should feel free to elaborate on the information provided above and add detail. Grafton's description should be merely a starting point.

D. After fifteen to twenty minutes, your instructor will call you back for a class discussion.

E. Answer the following questions:

1. What information that you collected do you think would be the most helpful in planning with a client such as Grafton?

2. What information was the most difficult to obtain?

3. What were your feelings about doing the interview, either as client or worker?

4. What did you learn about assessment from participating in this role play?

72

Chapter 5 Competencies/Practice Behaviors Exercises Assessment:

Name: _____ **Date:** _____

Supervisor's Name: _____

Focus Competencies/Practice Behaviors:
- EP 2.1.1c   Attend to professional roles and boundaries
- EP 2.1.1e   Engage in career-long learning
- EP 2.1.3   Apply critical thinking to inform and communicate professional judgments
- EP 2.1.7a   Utilize conceptual frameworks to guide the process of assessment, intervention, and evaluation
- EP 2.1.10   Engage, assess, intervene, and evaluate with individuals, families, groups, organizations, and communities
- EP 2.1.10d   Collect, organize, and interpret client data
- EP 2.1.10e   Assess client strengths and limitations

Instructions:

A.   Evaluate your work or your partner's work in the Focus Competencies/Practice Behaviors by completing the Competencies/Practice Behaviors Assessment form below

B.   What other Competencies/Practice Behaviors did you use to complete these Exercises? Be sure to record them in your assessments

1.	I have attained this competency/practice behavior (in the range of 81 to 100%)
2.	I have largely attained this competency/practice behavior (in the range of 61 to 80%)
3.	I have partially attained this competency/practice behavior (in the range of 41 to 60%)
4.	I have made a little progress in attaining this competency/practice behavior (in the range of 21 to 40%)
5.	I have made almost no progress in attaining this competency/practice behavior (in the range of 0 to 20%)

EPAS 2008 Core Competencies & Core Practice Behaviors	Student Self Assessment						Evaluator Feedback
Student and Evaluator Assessment Scale and Comments	0	1	2	3	4	5	**Agree/Disagree/Comments**
EP 2.1.1 Identify as a Professional Social Worker and Conduct Oneself Accordingly:							
a. Advocate for client access to the services of social work							
b. Practice personal reflection and self-correction to assure continual professional development							
c. Attend to professional roles and boundaries							
d. Demonstrate professional demeanor in behavior, appearance, and communication							
e. Engage in career-long learning							
f. Use supervision and consultation							
EP 2.1.2 Apply Social Work Ethical Principles to Guide Professional Practice:							
a. Recognize and manage personal values in a way that allows professional values to guide practice							
b. Make ethical decisions by applying NASW Code of Ethics and, as applicable, of the IFSW/IASSW Ethics in Social Work, Statement of Principles							

c.	Tolerate ambiguity in resolving ethical conflicts					
d.	Apply strategies of ethical reasoning to arrive at principled decisions					
EP 2.1.3 Apply Critical Thinking to Inform and Communicate Professional Judgments:						
a.	Distinguish, appraise, and integrate multiple sources of knowledge, including research-based knowledge and practice wisdom					
b.	Analyze models of assessment, prevention, intervention, and evaluation					
c.	Demonstrate effective oral and written communication in working with individuals, families, groups, organizations, communities, and colleagues					
EP 2.1.4 Engage Diversity and Difference in Practice:						
a.	Recognize the extent to which a culture's structures and values may oppress, marginalize, alienate, or create or enhance privilege and power					
b.	Gain sufficient self-awareness to eliminate the influence of personal biases and values in working with diverse groups					
c.	Recognize and communicate their understanding of the importance of difference in shaping life experiences					
d.	View themselves as learners and engage those with whom they work as informants					
EP 2.1.5 Advance Human Rights and Social and Economic Justice:						
a.	Understand forms and mechanisms of oppression and discrimination					
b.	Advocate for human rights and social and economic justice					
c.	Engage in practices that advance social and economic justice					
EP 2.1.6 Engage in Research-Informed Practice and Practice-Informed Research:						
a.	Use practice experience to inform scientific inquiry					
b.	Use research evidence to inform practice					
EP 2.1.7 Apply Knowledge of Human Behavior and the Social Environment:						
a.	Utilize conceptual frameworks to guide the processes of assessment, intervention, and evaluation					
b.	Critique and apply knowledge to understand person and environment					
EP 2.1.8 Engage in Policy Practice to Advance Social and Economic Well-Being and to Deliver Effective Social Work Services:						
a.	Analyze, formulate, and advocate for policies that advance social well-being					
b.	Collaborate with colleagues and clients for effective policy action					
EP 2.1.9 Respond to Contexts that Shape Practice:						
a.	Continuously discover, appraise, and attend to changing locales, populations, scientific and technological developments, and emerging societal trends to provide relevant services					

74

b.	Provide leadership in promoting sustainable changes in service delivery and practice to improve the quality of social services						
EP 2.1.10 Engage, Assess, Intervene, and Evaluate with Individuals, Families, Groups, Organizations and Communities:							
a.	Substantively and affectively prepare for action with individuals, families, groups, organizations, and communities						
b.	Use empathy and other interpersonal skills						
c.	Develop a mutually agreed-on focus of work and desired outcomes						
d.	Collect, organize, and interpret client data						
e.	Assess client strengths and limitations						
f.	Develop mutually agreed-on intervention goals and objectives						
g.	Select appropriate intervention strategies						
h.	Initiate actions to achieve organizational goals						
i.	Implement prevention interventions that enhance client capacities						
j.	Help clients resolve problems						
k.	Negotiate, mediate, and advocate for clients						
l.	Facilitate transitions and endings						
m.	Critically analyze, monitor, and evaluate interventions						

Competencies/Practice Behaviors Exercise 6.1
Prioritizing Problems

Focus Competencies or Practice Behaviors:

- EP 2.1.3   Apply critical thinking to inform and communicate professional judgments
- EP 2.1.10   Engage, assess, intervene, and evaluate with individuals, families, groups, organizations, and communities
- EP 2.1.10c   Develop a mutually agreed-on focus of work and desired outcomes
- EP 2.1.10e   Assess client strengths and limitations
- EP 2.1.10f   Develop mutually agreed-on intervention goals and objectives

Instructions:

A.   Before beginning this exercise, review the material in the text on the steps in the planning process. The planning process is summarized in the accompanying diagram. This exercise will be done with another classmate.

B.   Take a sheet of scratch paper and vertically list the letters *a* through *e*. Beside each letter, cite a problem you are currently having. Problems may range from the very broad (for example, not having any money or being depressed) to the very specific (for instance, setting up two different dates at the same time next Thursday night or forgetting to send your mother a birthday card). Do *not* list problems that you don't care to share (for example, you think you're pregnant). You will be asked to share the list of problems with your partner.

C.   Break up into pairs. Take turns playing the worker and the client. First, the worker asks the client about his or her problems for approximately fifteen minutes. The worker should:

       a.   Identify with the client the range of problems that are most significant to the client. (Problems should be included only when the client recognizes their significance, they can be clearly defined, and there is some possibility of finding a solution.)

       b.   Restate each problem using explicit behavioral terms.

       c.   Prioritize the problems in order of their importance to the client.

D.   After fifteen minutes, reverse roles and do the same thing.

E.   Discuss the following questions and issues:

       1.   How difficult was it to identify problems? Explain.

2.   How difficult was it to use explicit behavioral terms? Explain.

3.   How difficult was it to prioritize the array of problems? Explain.

4.   What problems tended to take highest priority (for example, the most serious, the simplest, or the easiest to solve)?

5.   How similar do you think this exercise is to prioritizing problems with real clients?

PLANNING IN THE GENERALIST INTERVENTION MODEL

FOUNDATION FOR GENERALIST PRACTICE

Knowledge   *Skills*   *Values*

ENGAGEMENT

ASSESSMENT

PLANNING

STEP 1: **Work with the client.**

STEP 2: **Prioritize problems.**

PROBLEM
1.
2.
3. etc.

STEP 3: **Translate problems into needs.**

Problem	→	*Need*
1.	→	1.
2.	→	2.
3.	→	3. etc.

STEP 4: **Evaluate levels of intervention for each need.**

NEED #1: _____ etc.

a. Identify Alternatives: → b. Propose Solutions → c. Evaluate:

	a. Identify Alternatives:	b. Propose Solutions	*Pros*	*Cons*	*Client Strengths*
MICRO					
MEZZO					
MACRO					

STEP 5: **Establish primary goals.**

STEP 6: **Specify objectives.**

	Who?	Will do what?	By when?	How will you measure success?
1.				
2.				
3.				

STEP 7: **Formalize a contract.**

78

Focus Competencies or Practice Behaviors:

- EP 2.1.3   Apply critical thinking to inform and communicate professional judgments
- EP 2.1.10c   Develop a mutually agreed-on focus of work and desired outcomes
- EP 2.1.10e   Assess client strengths and limitations
- EP 2.1.10f   Develop mutually agreed-on intervention goals and objectives

Instructions:

A.   Review the material in the text concerning translating problems into needs.
B.   By yourself, translate the following problems into needs:

Problem	**Need(s)**
1) Truancy	_____
2) Children don't listen	_____
3) Spouses are unable to communicate	_____
4) No resources for paying the rent	_____
5) Infertility	_____
6) Wife is battered almost daily	_____
7) Sexual harassment at work	_____
8) Being HIV positive	_____
9) Severe developmental disability	_____
10) Unwanted pregnancy	_____
11) Racial discrimination at work	_____
12) Rheumatoid arthritis	_____
13) Runaway adolescent son	_____
14) Cocaine addiction	_____
15) Divorced spouse not paying support	_____
16) Violent teen gang in neighborhood	_____
17) Received drunk driving ticket	_____
18) "Stuck" in minimum wage job	_____

79

C.   Afterwards, address the following questions:

1.   Which problems were the most difficult to translate into needs? What were the reasons for this?

2.   Which problems needed further clarification and why?

3.   How do needs provide clues for what services might be useful?

Competencies/Practice Behaviors Exercise 6.3
Clarifying Vague Objectives

Focus Competencies or Practice Behaviors:
- EP 2.1.3   Apply critical thinking to inform and communicate professional judgments
- EP 2.1.10f   Develop mutually agreed-on intervention goals and objectives

Instructions:
A.   Review the material in the text concerning establishing goals and objectives.
B.   In a class discussion, or on your own, address the vague objective statements given below, one by one. Discuss the reasons why each statement is vague and establish improved objective statements. Use the performance/conditions/standards formula discussed in the text to formulate new objectives. Finally, clearly identify what portions of the new objectives reflect performance, conditions, and standards.

80

Vague Objective Statement	Reasons for Vagueness	Improved Restatement: Performance/Conditions/Standards
1. Promote emotional well-being	_____ _____ _____	_____ _____ _____
2. Increase self-awareness	_____ _____ _____	_____ _____ _____
3. Find adequate housing	_____ _____ _____	_____ _____ _____
4. Facilitate adequate functioning	_____ _____ _____	_____ _____ _____
5. Accept physical disability	_____ _____ _____	_____ _____ _____
6. Dress appropriately	_____ _____ _____	_____ _____ _____
7. Increase motivation	_____ _____ _____	_____ _____ _____
8. Show interest	_____ _____ _____	_____ _____ _____

9. Respond appropriately   _____   _____

_____   _____

_____   _____

10. Improve self-concept   _____   _____

_____   _____

_____   _____

11. Develop a relationship   _____   _____

_____   _____

_____   _____

12. Decrease hostile attitude   _____   _____

_____   _____

Competencies/Practice Behaviors Exercise 6.4
Role-Play: Making a Contract

Focus Competencies or Practice Behaviors:
- EP 2.1.10c   Develop a mutually agreed-on focus of work and desired outcomes
- EP 2.1.10f   Develop mutually agreed-on intervention goals and objectives

Instructions:
A.   Review the material in the text on formalizing a contract.
B.   In preparation for a role play, read about the following characters:

Role Play Characters
Lucinda, sixteen, is referred to the Oconomowoc County Social Services Department by a local hospital. She just delivered Rosanna there two days ago and doesn't know what to do or where to go. Her parents, Frannie and Darryl, refuse to let her come home. They insist that she give the baby up for adoption. Lucinda adamantly refuses. Lucinda, a high school junior, is a C+ student. She has never presented her parents with major behavioral problems before her pregnancy. Gavin, seventeen, Rosanna's father, wants nothing to do with the situation and has not been in contact with Lucinda for five months.

Frannie, thirty-eight, Lucinda's mother, is distraught by her daughter's "sinful" behavior. She doesn't want Lucinda to "ruin her life" by giving up her childhood to be a mother herself. She feels that if she refuses to let Lucinda come home, she will force her daughter to give the baby up for adoption because she lacks other options. Frannie does not want "to start all over again" and help Lucinda with the many parenting tasks Frannie knows are involved. Frannie is very outspoken about her feelings.

Darryl, forty-four, Lucinda's father, agrees with Frannie, although less adamantly. On the one hand, he wants Lucinda to give Rosanna up. On the other, he loves his daughter dearly and worries both about what she will do now and about how she will feel in the future about losing Rosanna. However, he tends to be cowed by Frannie's strong will and volatile temperament. Darryl finds it much easier to agree with Frannie than to fight her, especially on major issues such as this.

The Worker, Ms. DeWitt, is an intake worker at the Oconomowoc County Department of Social Services. Her job is to work with initial referrals and establish beginning plans of action. Ms. DeWitt has read the initial referral information and has spoken with all three family members on the phone. This is her first face-to-face meeting with them. She needs to help Lucinda, Frannie, and Darryl come to some agreement and establish an initial contract regarding what they will do about Rosanna. She feels that foster placement is a viable temporary solution until the family can come to a decision concerning Rosanna's permanent placement. Rosanna remains temporarily at the hospital.

C. Volunteers are needed to play the various roles. They should assume places in the front of the class where other class members can easily see them. The worker's task is to establish an initial contract with the family following the "Contract for Intervention Plan" cited below. Note that the number of objectives can vary. The role play should last no longer than twenty minutes.

Contract for Intervention Plan

Client Name: _____

I.   Brief description of the problem:

II.   Primary goals:

III.   Objectives:
        A.   _____
        B.   _____
        C.   _____
        D.   _____

_____
(Signature of Worker)   (Date)

_____
(Signature[s] of Client[s])   (Date)
_____
_____

D.	The class should observe the role play until a contract is established or twenty minutes have passed (whichever comes first). The instructor should record on the blackboard the contract as it has been developed so that it's easier to discuss, even if the contract has not yet been completed. Discussion will focus on the following questions and issues:

1.	Summarize what occurred during the role play.

2.	What difficulties did the worker encounter?

3.	To what extent are the objectives clearly stated?

4.	What did you learn from the role play that you might be able to apply to contracting with your own clients in practice?

84

Chapter 6 Competencies/Practice Behaviors Exercises Assessment:

Name: _____ **Date:** _____
Supervisor's Name: _____

Focus Competencies/Practice Behaviors:

- EP 2.1.3   Apply critical thinking to inform and communicate professional judgments
- EP 2.1.10   Engage, assess, intervene, and evaluate with individuals, families, groups, organizations, and communities
- EP 2.1.10c   Develop a mutually agreed-on focus of work and desired outcomes
- EP 2.1.10e   Assess client strengths and limitations
- EP 2.1.10f   Develop mutually agreed-on intervention goals and objectives

Instructions:

A.   Evaluate your work or your partner's work in the Focus Competencies/Practice Behaviors by completing the Competencies/Practice Behaviors Assessment form below

B.   What other Competencies/Practice Behaviors did you use to complete these Exercises? Be sure to record them in your assessments

1.	I have attained this competency/practice behavior (in the range of 81 to 100%)
2.	I have largely attained this competency/practice behavior (in the range of 61 to 80%)
3.	I have partially attained this competency/practice behavior (in the range of 41 to 60%)
4.	I have made a little progress in attaining this competency/practice behavior (in the range of 21 to 40%)
5.	I have made almost no progress in attaining this competency/practice behavior (in the range of 0 to 20%)

EPAS 2008 Core Competencies & Core Practice Behaviors				Student Self Assessment			Evaluator Feedback
Student and Evaluator Assessment Scale and Comments	0	1	2	3	4	5	Agree/Disagree/Comments
EP 2.1.1 Identify as a Professional Social Worker and Conduct Oneself Accordingly:							
a. Advocate for client access to the services of social work							
b. Practice personal reflection and self-correction to assure continual professional development							
c. Attend to professional roles and boundaries							
d. Demonstrate professional demeanor in behavior, appearance, and communication							
e. Engage in career-long learning							
f. Use supervision and consultation							
EP 2.1.2 Apply Social Work Ethical Principles to Guide Professional Practice:							
a. Recognize and manage personal values in a way that allows professional values to guide practice							
b. Make ethical decisions by applying NASW Code of Ethics and, as applicable, of the IFSW/IASSW Ethics in Social Work, Statement of Principles							
c. Tolerate ambiguity in resolving ethical conflicts							

85

d. Apply strategies of ethical reasoning to arrive at principled decisions							

EP 2.1.3 Apply Critical Thinking to Inform and Communicate Professional Judgments:							
a. Distinguish, appraise, and integrate multiple sources of knowledge, including research-based knowledge and practice wisdom							
b. Analyze models of assessment, prevention, intervention, and evaluation							
c. Demonstrate effective oral and written communication in working with individuals, families, groups, organizations, communities, and colleagues							

EP 2.1.4 Engage Diversity and Difference in Practice:							
a. Recognize the extent to which a culture's structures and values may oppress, marginalize, alienate, or create or enhance privilege and power							
b. Gain sufficient self-awareness to eliminate the influence of personal biases and values in working with diverse groups							
c. Recognize and communicate their understanding of the importance of difference in shaping life experiences							
d. View themselves as learners and engage those with whom they work as informants							

EP 2.1.5 Advance Human Rights and Social and Economic Justice:							
a. Understand forms and mechanisms of oppression and discrimination							
b. Advocate for human rights and social and economic justice							
c. Engage in practices that advance social and economic justice							

EP 2.1.6 Engage in Research-Informed Practice and Practice-Informed Research:							
a. Use practice experience to inform scientific inquiry							
b. Use research evidence to inform practice							

EP 2.1.7 Apply Knowledge of Human Behavior and the Social Environment:							
a. Utilize conceptual frameworks to guide the processes of assessment, intervention, and evaluation							
b. Critique and apply knowledge to understand person and environment							

EP 2.1.8 Engage in Policy Practice to Advance Social and Economic Well-Being and to Deliver Effective Social Work Services:							
a. Analyze, formulate, and advocate for policies that advance social well-being							
b. Collaborate with colleagues and clients for effective policy action							

EP 2.1.9 Respond to Contexts that Shape Practice:							
a. Continuously discover, appraise, and attend to changing locales, populations, scientific and technological developments, and emerging societal trends to provide relevant services							

b. Provide leadership in promoting sustainable changes in service delivery and practice to improve the quality of social services							
EP 2.1.10 Engage, Assess, Intervene, and Evaluate with Individuals, Families, Groups, Organizations and Communities:							
a. Substantively and affectively prepare for action with individuals, families, groups, organizations, and communities							
b. Use empathy and other interpersonal skills							
c. Develop a mutually agreed-on focus of work and desired outcomes							
d. Collect, organize, and interpret client data							
e. Assess client strengths and limitations							
f. Develop mutually agreed-on intervention goals and objectives							
g. Select appropriate intervention strategies							
h. Initiate actions to achieve organizational goals							
i. Implement prevention interventions that enhance client capacities							
j. Help clients resolve problems							
k. Negotiate, mediate, and advocate for clients							
l. Facilitate transitions and endings							
m. Critically analyze, monitor, and evaluate interventions							

Competencies/Practice Behaviors Exercise 7.1
Risk Management

Focus Competencies or Practice Behaviors:
- EP 2.1.7a   Utilize conceptual frameworks to guide the process of assessment, intervention, and evaluation
- EP 2.1.10a   Substantively and affectively prepare for action with individuals, families, groups, organizations, and communities
- EP 2.1.10g   Select appropriate intervention strategies

Instructions:
A.   Prior to doing this exercise, review the material in the text on risk management in protective services.

B.   Assessment of the five forces of risk is an integral part of the risk management process. You will be asked to assess these forces (maltreatment, child, parent, family, and intervention) in the Ashton case situation.[1]

The Ashton Case[2]

The Presenting Problem

A concerned neighbor calls Milwaukee County Protective Services to report that Tiffany Ashton is abusing her eight-year-old daughter Dominique. A Protective Services worker named Ms. Stalwart reviews Ms. Ashton's records and visits the Ashton home to investigate the situation.

Ms. Stalwart finds Ms. Ashton extremely disoriented and depressed. Her sister recently died in a car accident due to her being drunk while driving. Apparently, this seriously affected Ms. Ashton's emotional stability. Ms. Stalwart takes Ms. Ashton to a Milwaukee Public Hospital and places Dominique in emergency foster care until Ms. Ashton's mental health improves.

Prior Agency History

Agency records indicate that nine months ago, Dominique's teacher had referred Dominique to Protective Services because she missed eight consecutive days of school without an excuse. The school could not reach Ms. Ashton by phone to find out what was wrong. Dominique's teacher indicated that Dominique's school performance has increasingly deteriorated over the past several months.

A Protective Services worker visited the home and found no evidence of habitation. A next-door neighbor indicated that Ms. Ashton and Dominique hadn't been around for several weeks. She said they had moved in with Ms. Ashton's boyfriend, Jagger, in a small flat a block away. The neighbor gave the worker the new address.

---

[1] The five forces of risk and suggestions for their evaluation are based on that described in *Child Protective Services Risk Management: A Decision-making Handbook* (1991). Charlotte, NC: Action for Child Protection, developed by Holder and Corey.

[2] This case is based loosely on a case study entitled "Case History #3: The Heller Family," in *Resource Materials: A Curriculum on Child Abuse and Neglect,* published by the U.S. Department of Health, Education, and Welfare, DHEW Publication No. (OHDS) 79-30221, 1979.

When the worker arrived at Jagger's apartment, Ms. Ashton appeared surprised but allowed her in to talk. The worker noted that Dominique had numerous bruises on her arms and legs. Ms. Ashton acknowledged that she had beaten Dominique with a stick three days earlier. Ms. Ashton continued that the beating resulted from Dominique starting a fire in her bedroom while Ms. Ashton and Jagger were out. Ms. Ashton said she had been so shocked that she beat Dominique to emphasize how dangerous firesetting was. Ms. Ashton and Jagger often left Dominique alone to fend for herself when they were gone.

After a number of interviews, the Protective Services worker determined that the beating was a singular occurrence. Furthermore, Ms. Ashton regretted the beating deeply and expressed eagerness to cooperate with the worker. Ms. Ashton evidently did not understand that leaving an eight-year-old daughter alone for substantial periods of time was inappropriate and potentially dangerous. Ms. Ashton indicated that in the future she would make certain she found a babysitter before going out.

Four months later (and five months before Ms. Stalwart found her disoriented in her apartment), Ms. Ashton tried to kill herself by taking an overdose of sleeping pills. After she had spent several days in the hospital, her physician referred her to the local mental health center for treatment. However, she never followed through on this recommendation.

Two months later (and three months before Ms. Stalwart found her), Jagger beat Ms. Ashton up and threw her out of his apartment. She returned to her current apartment.

Prior Family History

Ms. Ashton's own personal history was turbulent. She was one of nine children raised in a poverty-stricken, multiproblem family. Her parents were alcoholics. They were divorced after her father was found guilty of committing incest with two of her sisters. Subsequently, Ms. Ashton and several of her siblings were removed from the home and placed in foster care for several years.

After becoming pregnant at age seventeen, she married Dominique's father, who deserted her shortly thereafter. She contemplated giving Dominique up for adoption but decided against it. She never divorced Dominique's father because she still "really loves him." She became pregnant twice more with different boyfriends and gave both children up for adoption.

Since Dominique's birth, Ms. Ashton has been receiving public assistance. At Ms. Ashton's request, the County Department of Social Services enrolled her in three job training programs over the years. However, she soon dropped out of each, and so never neared completion. She experienced several bouts of depression for which she received medication. Until Dominique was three, Ms. Ashton lived with her own prior foster parents who provided Dominique with satisfactory care.

Dominique's History

Dominique achieved her developmental milestones within normal limits. Her childhood was healthy with the exception of common childhood diseases.

Dominique's teachers describe Dominique as a pleasant, likable child. However, she does poorly in school, especially in math and English. They indicate that Dominique has been seriously distressed by her mother's mental state, which has detracted from Dominique's school performance.

A recent report by a consulting psychologist indicates that, despite Ms. Ashton's emotional difficulties, she and Dominique have a "close, loving relationship." They care deeply for each other and, according to his recommendation, should not be permanently separated.

1. Address the questions relating to each force, note those areas where you need additional information, and arbitrarily evaluate the amount of risk you feel is present. Subsequently, evaluate the risk for each force as great, moderate, or small.

It is beyond the scope of this workbook to undertake an extensive risk assessment as a worker would conduct in real life. This exercise is designed to help you focus on those variables contributing to risk in any particular family and make an arbitrary judgment about what should be done. In a real case situation, the assessment would assume much greater depth.

---

a. *Maltreatment Force* involves the types and severity of maltreatment that are occurring in the home, and the conditions under which maltreatment usually occurs.

   1) Are the children being neglected, burned, beaten, or sexually molested?

   2) Is the abusive parent drunk, depressed, or explosive?

   3) Does the maltreatment occur randomly or only in times of crisis?

   4) What amount of risk does maltreatment force generate within the home—great, moderate, or small?

b. *Child Force* involves the maltreated child's personal characteristics and the extent to which you as the worker perceive the child as being susceptible to maltreatment.

   1) Is Dominique extremely withdrawn, brashly aggressive, or exceptionally slow to respond?

   2) Is Dominique a very young child or physically disabled (which would make her exceptionally vulnerable)?

   3) What amount of risk does child force generate within the home—great, moderate, or small?

c. *Parent Force* entails the characteristics of parents in the family, the parents' child management skills, the parents' own upbringing and past experiences, and the interactional patterns of the parents with others.

   1) *Ms. Ashton's Characteristics:*

     a) How does Ms. Ashton feel about herself?

     b) Does she feel guilty after maltreatment occurs?

     c) How does she cope with external stresses?

   2) *Ms. Ashton's Parenting Skills:*

     a) To what extent does Ms. Ashton rely on physical punishment to control Dominique?

     b) How responsive is Ms. Ashton to Dominique's wants and demands?

   3) *Ms. Ashton's Own Upbringing:*

     a) How was Ms. Ashton treated by her own parents?

     b) Do they have a prison record or record of legal convictions?

     c) Do they have health difficulties?

   4) *Ms. Ashton's Parents' Interactions:*

     a) How do Ms. Ashton's parents communicate with other people?

     b) Do they have friends or neighbors with whom they associate?

     c) To what extent are they isolated from others?

In summary, what amount of risk does parent force generate within the home—great, moderate, or small?

---

d. *Family Force* concerns family demographics, family functioning and communication, and the overall support and nurturance the family receives from the surrounding social environment.

   1) *Family Demographics*:
      a) What variables characterize the family in terms of demographics?
      b) Are one or both parents involved?
      c) How many children are there?
      d) Is the family a blended stepfamily?
      e) What levels of education, job training, and work experience do the parents have?
      f) What is the family's income level?
      g) Is unemployment a problem?
      h) What are their housing conditions like?

   2) *Family Function and Communication:*
      If the parents are married, how do they get along?
      a) How involved is Jagger or other boyfriends with Dominique?
      b) How do family members talk to each other?
      c) How would you describe the family's lifestyle?
      d) Is the family prone to crises?

   3) *Environmental Supports*
      a) What relationships does the family have with extended family members?
      b) Does the family have access to adequate transportation?
      c) Is the family socially isolated?

   In summary, what amount of risk does family force generate within the home—great, moderate, or small?

2. Now address the following questions:
   a. What do you feel is the overall amount of risk to Dominique in the Ashton home—great, moderate, or small?

   b. In a real treatment situation, what types of goals might you as a worker pursue? Consider the following (Berry, 2005; Crosson-Tower, 2005; Holder & Cary, 1991):
      1) *Self-Sufficiency*
         Parents and families frequently need to enhance their ability to function independently. This dimension has to do with families being better able to fend for themselves and satisfy their own needs. Specific objectives often involve increasing self-esteem and confidence.
      2) *Communication Skills*
         Goals focusing on improved communication skills among family members are common. Members can be encouraged to identify and express their feelings openly and honestly. Listening skills can be enhanced. Family members' ability to understand each other's point of view can be improved.
      3) *Parenting Knowledge*
         Parents may not know how to handle and control children. They may have been brought up in emotionally deprived environments themselves. They may resort to force for controlling children's behavior because they've never been taught any other behavior management techniques.

91

They can be taught not only to control, but to play with and enjoy their children.

Additionally, parents may need knowledge about normal development. They need to know what to expect in terms of normal behavior at each age level. Appropriate expectations may reduce the frustrations parents feel when children don't behave the way the parents think they *should*.

4) *Stress Management*

Parents can be taught to better manage their stress levels. They can be taught to release their feelings more appropriately, instead of allowing emotional pressure to build up and explode. Learning specific stress management techniques such as relaxation approaches can also help them cope with stress.

5) *Impulse Control*

Many parents in families at risk have poor impulse control. They are under tremendous stress. They often need to learn how to direct their energies in more fruitful ways than by violently lashing out at children.

6) *Problem-Solving Skills*

Parents in high-risk families may be so frustrated and stressed that they feel they have little control over their lives and their behavior. They can be taught how to analyze problems, translate these problems into needs, establish potential alternatives for meeting these needs, evaluate the pros and cons of alternatives, and, finally, select and pursue their most promising options.

7) *Interactive Nurturing*

Many times family members need to be taught how to express their positive feelings, on the one hand, and accept affection, on the other. They can be taught how to empathize with each other, verbalize their feelings, and, hence, reinforce their support and caring for each other.

8) *Resource Enhancement*

A primary means of increasing the strength of families at risk is to increase their resources. Adequate employment, income, housing, food, and clothing all contribute to a family's wellbeing.

Competencies/Practice Behaviors Exercise 7.2
Spirituality As Strength

Focus Competencies or Practice Behaviors:
- EP 2.1.2a   Recognize and manage personal values in a way that allows professional values to guide practice
- EP 2.1.4b   Gain sufficient self-awareness to eliminate the influence of personal biases and values in working with diverse groups

Instructions:
A.   Before beginning this exercise, review the material on spirituality and religion as potential sources of strength for older adults (and others including yourself).
B.   Answer the questions posed on the questionnaire below.

Questionnaire: Your Personal Perceptions of Spirituality as a Potential Source of Strength

   1.   How would you differentiate spirituality from religion?

   2.   What are your personal beliefs about spirituality and religion as they apply to your own life?

   3.   What level of involvement, if any, do you have with a religious institution such as a church, synagogue, or mosque?

   4.   What role, if any, do you see this institution as having in supporting you in your daily and spiritual life?

   5.   How important, if at all, is this affiliation to you?

   6.   How would you describe your own philosophy of life?

   7.   What helps you most when you are afraid or need special help?

8.   What do you feel is most meaningful to you in your life at this time?

9.   What gives you hope for the future?

C.   Now, answer the following questions:

1.   In summary, to what extent do you perceive spirituality and religion as a potential source of strength?

2.   To what extent do you think spirituality and religion might serve as a potential source of strength to clients?

3.   How difficult do you feel it might be for you not to impose your own beliefs on your clients?

4.   What approaches might help you separate your own beliefs from those of your clients?

Focus Competencies or Practice Behaviors:
- EP 2.1.1c   Attend to professional roles and boundaries
- EP 2.1.1d   Demonstrate professional demeanor in behavior, appearance, and communication
- EP 2.1.3b   Analyze models of assessment, prevention, intervention, and evaluation
- EP 2.1.3c   Demonstrate effective oral and written communication in working with individuals, families, groups, organizations, communities, and colleagues
- EP 2.1.10a   Substantively and affectively prepare for action with individuals, families, groups, organizations, and communities
- EP 2.1.10b   Use empathy and other interpersonal skills
- EP 2.1.10c   Develop a mutually agreed-on focus of work and desired outcomes
- EP 2.1.10d   Collect, organize, and interpret client data
- EP 2.1.10e   Assess client strengths and limitations
- EP 2.1.10f   Develop mutually agreed-on intervention goals and objectives
- EP 2.1.10j   Help clients resolve problems

Instructions:
A.   Before beginning this exercise, review the material in the text on crisis intervention.
B.   Volunteers are needed to participate in a role play involving crisis intervention. Otherwise, your instructor will assign roles. The roles are as follows:

Role Play: Crisis Intervention

Social Work Role: Two social workers are intake workers in a crisis intervention unit of a community mental health center. Their job is to meet with people who phone for help because of a current crisis, assess the situation, and make the appropriate referrals. They have already gathered the following information about the clients.

The Situation: The workers are meeting with Farrah, Francine, and Felicity. Farrah's husband, Festus, was killed in a car accident five weeks earlier. Francine, sixteen, and Felicity, twelve, are Farrah's daughters. One other child, Fulbert, four, is not present at the interview.

Farrah, thirty-four, had been happily married to Festus for eighteen years. Having married right after high school, she has never worked outside the home. She loves her children very much and is very concerned about what will happen to them now.

     Farrah is a quiet, pleasant, soft-spoken woman who is overwhelmed with grief and with the terror of being alone. She loved Festus dearly and had a very close relationship with him. He tended to make most of the family's decisions. Farrah had gone from being dependent on her parents to being dependent on Festus. She felt relatively comfortable and settled in that role.

     Festus, thirty-eight, had been an assistant at the Morbid Misty Eye Mortuary for the past seventeen years. He had been earning $42,000 per year.

     The family has a small home with only ten years remaining on the mortgage at 9 percent interest. Although the family had never been wealthy, they had lived comfortably and adequately. Farrah was exceptionally good at managing the household finances. Now Farrah has the following major concerns:
     1.   Grief at the loss of her husband.
     2.   Fear of loneliness.

---

3. Financial worries—house payments, food, clothing, etc.
4. Worry about the children—both their emotional and physical needs.
5. What she will do.

Francine (nicknamed Foofy), sixteen, is an outgoing, friendly young woman who maintains a B+ average in school. She is fairly well adjusted in school, participates in a number of class activities (including cheerleading and chess club), and has many friends.

Francine is suffering from terrible grief at the loss of her father. She had a very good relationship with him and misses him very much.

It seems things in her life have gone pretty well up until now. But now everything has fallen apart. She doesn't know what to do. She's worried about her mother and siblings. She doesn't know what will happen to the family. It seems her father was always the strong one who held things together. She can't even concentrate on her schoolwork much anymore. She'd like to help her mother, but just doesn't know what to do.

In summary, Francine has the following major concerns:
1. Grief at the loss of her father.
2. Questions about what her mother is going to do now.
3. Worry over her siblings and what will happen to them.
4. Worry about what will happen to her.

Felicity, twelve, is a pretty yet shy and withdrawn girl. She lacks self-confidence and generally has had difficulties in school, both with grades and with making friends.

She, too, is very upset by her father's death. She feels he was the only family member she could talk to.

Felicity feels that Francine, unlike herself, always seems to do well and have things come easily for her. Felicity resents this and often finds herself becoming angry at Francine. She feels guilty about these negative feelings toward her sister.

Felicity loves her mother but feels that her mother sides with Francine on most issues. Felicity especially resents how her mother tends to speak for her and answer questions addressed to her.

In summary, Felicity has the following major concerns:
1. Grief at the loss of her father.
2. Resentment towards her sister Francine for "being better at everything" than she is.
3. Resentment towards her mother Farrah for never listening to her opinion.
4. Low levels of self-confidence.
5. Lack of friends.

C. Volunteers should seat themselves in front of the class where they can be observed easily. Each volunteer should display an 8" x 5" note card with the client name marked boldly so that observers can better remember which volunteer is playing which role.

D. The workers should focus on the planning and intervention steps in the crisis intervention model presented in the text. Assessment, of course, is an ongoing process. The role play should continue for twenty to thirty minutes. Your instructor will indicate to the role players when it's time to stop.

E. During the role play, observers should take notes on the form shown below as they address the following questions:

Role Play Feedback Form

A.   What do you think are particularly *good techniques* used by the social workers? How did the *clients react* to these techniques? (Please be specific.)

B.   Do you see any weaknesses or areas in which improvement would be helpful? (Specific suggestions for how to improve are beneficial.)

C.   Do you have any additional thoughts or comments?

F.   After the role play, answer the following questions:

1.   What feedback did you note on your feedback forms? Strengths? Suggestions for improvement? Other comments?

2.   What did you feel were the critical points in the role play?

3.   To what extent did you feel the workers followed and applied the steps inherent in crisis intervention?

4.   How did the workers feel while doing the role play?

5.   How did the clients feel in reaction to what the workers said?

Competencies/Practice Behaviors Exercise 7.4
Role-Play: What Do You Do with a Drunken Sailor (or an Alcoholic Client)?

Focus Competencies or Practice Behaviors:
- EP 2.1.3c   Demonstrate effective oral and written communication in working with individuals, families, groups, organizations, communities, and colleagues
- EP 2.1.7b   Critique and apply knowledge to understand person and environment
- EP 2.1.10a   Substantively and affectively prepare for action with individuals, families, groups, organizations, and communities
- EP 2.1.10b   Use empathy and other interpersonal skills
- EP 2.1.10d   Collect, organize, and interpret client data
- EP 2.1.10e   Assess client strengths and limitations
- EP 2.1.10f   Develop mutually agreed-on intervention goals and objectives
- EP 2.1.10g   Select appropriate intervention strategies
- EP 2.1.10j   Help clients resolve problems

98

Instructions:

A.   Before beginning this exercise, review the material on alcohol and other drug abuse presented in the text.

B.   Volunteers are needed to play the various roles cited below. Your instructor will first read them to you.

Roles

Stephanie, twenty-one, is a college junior who majors in education and loves to "party." She has been known to label herself a "party animal." She goes out drinking almost every night (after some studying, of course). She drank occasionally at parties during high school and even got drunk a dozen or two times. When she first got to college, she limited herself to going out and "getting plastered" only on Friday and Saturday nights. However, as time passed, she's found herself wanting to go out every night.

She has fun, all right. But twice last month she found herself waking up in bed with some guy she didn't remember ever seeing before. Those guys were pretty "sleazy-looking," too. How embarrassing! Each time she surely got out of there in a hurry. She hopes she remembered to use condoms.

After all, she's doing okay in school. Sure, her grades have slumped a little bit. She's dropped from a B+ to a straight C average. But that's because the older she gets, the more difficult her courses get. For example, that stats course is pure misery. She often tells herself she's doing fine.

She's not crazy about the headaches she has most mornings. It takes her a while to get going. But she's only missed six or seven mornings of class since the semester started. She's doing okay. She surely isn't an alcoholic or anything like that.

The problem is that as she was driving from one bar to another the other night, a cop (who must've come out of the Twilight Zone because she surely didn't see him) busted her for drunk driving. Rats. What a bummer. What a fine. She also has to take a series of drug education courses. Crummy.

Carlo, thirty-three, works on the line at Darley Havidson Motorcycle Manufacturing Company making "hogs" (a slang term used by motorcycle enthusiasts to refer to "awesome" cycle machines.) He married Blair nine years ago after he "knocked her up." They now have four children whom he frequently refers to as "ye olde wailing brats." Sometimes, he thinks it's too bad he doesn't like children very much.

He works second shift so he doesn't have to see too much of the family. Blair works first shift at George Webb's hamburger parlor. Carlo sometimes thinks that people who work there are required to have bad complexions and a hundred extra pounds of fat. That's Blair, all right.

Carlo's one joy in life is going down to Heck's Tavern and having a few "brewski's" after work. He and his cronies inevitably close it down and stagger home. Carlo even volunteers for overtime whenever possible so he won't miss weekend nights. Otherwise, he contents himself with a few twelve-packs and TV (football when in season).

In a vague way, Carlo thinks he's not very happy with his life. But he doesn't like to think about it too much. It's too depressing. The job's boring and he's never completely sure he won't get laid off. Yet, he can't afford to quit and start over somewhere else. Blair's constantly "bitchin'" about his drinking when he does see her. She says he slaps her around when he's drunk. Maybe, just a little, but not much. It's a good thing they work different shifts.

Day after day, week after week, he waits patiently for closing time when he can "belt down a few" and forget all his humdrum problems.

99

The problem is that last week that crazy town cop gave him a drunk driving ticket as he was trying to drive home. Carlo wasn't really drunk. He only had a few beers. How do you expect a guy to be able to relax, anyhow?

Viki, fifty-seven, is an executive for an accounting firm. She's been married to Alex, a sixty-year-old engineering consultant, for thirty-four years. Their three adult children live with their own families in various peripheries of the country.

Viki's job is extremely demanding. She usually works eleven-hour days, often including weekends. Alex's job is also demanding, so they don't see much of each other. They never were much for socializing, anyway. In the free time he does have, Alex keeps busy with fishing, reading, and doing projects around the house.

Although Viki often states that she loves her job, she typically comes home exhausted. Her high-level position makes her feel very important. She feels she needs to keep striving for greater and greater accomplishments in order to keep up with her very competitive colleagues.

Upon entering the door as she gets home, Viki can't wait to mix her first very dry martini. Then she can't wait to mix her next one . . . and the next. Finally, after a couple of hours, she passes out on the couch watching television. Meanwhile, Alex goes to bed by himself. Viki will usually wake up at 2:00 or 3:00 a.m. and crawl into bed. A few hours later, her alarm sounds and she's soon off to work again.

Martinis help Viki relax. It's tough to "wind down" after a whirlwind day at the office. She's not an alcoholic, though. She only drinks to relax, and then only a few martinis.

The problem is, she had to attend a going-away party for one of her colleagues two weeks ago. She only had a couple of martinis. That cop must've been parked outside the bar where the party was held, just waiting for her to come out. Anyway, he gave her a ticket for drunk driving. How mortifying. And to think she usually only drinks a little at home.

Mortimer, sixteen, isn't into school very much. His parents are always on his back, so he does go. But they can't make him pay attention. He is passing. What do they want? He even got a C in shop last term.

Mortimer's got a part-time job, working after school at the local Sentry supermarket. It's not much of a job. It only pays minimum wage, but it does keep him in funny money.

Mortimer mostly likes to go out with his friends. They'll go to a game, watch TV, or "scope cherubs" (that is, look for gorgeous younger women who adore "older" men). Occasionally, he and his friends will really "get down and party heavy." Maybe every month or so, he'll really "tie one on." So what? He's just trying to have a little fun. He's only young once, right?

It worries him just a tad, however, how he can never remember what happened after a major party. He just wakes up the next morning with a major hangover to match. So what? It only happens once in a while. He's just having some fun. He doesn't *have* to drink. He just does it to have some fun with his friends.

The problem is that last Saturday morning, his dad entered his bedroom with the most somber expression on his face. Mortimer wondered how anybody could be beet red in anger and yet resemble a hard, cold stone statue like that. That's when his dad stated in a deathly, steel-like calm, icy voice, "How'd you annihilate the right front fender on the Lexus last night?"

"Oh, s _ _ _ _," Mortimer thought to himself. He didn't remember a thing.

C.   Using the suggestions for working with alcoholics and other drug abusers presented in the text, the remainder of the class should take turns approaching each client about his or her behavior and situation. Role players should be addressed in turn, one at a time. The discussion for each client should take about 10 minutes. Your instructor will tell you when it's time to talk to the next client.

Class members should ask questions and make comments targeting three aspects of the situation:
a.   Assessment of whether each role player is an alcoholic.
b.   Addressing the problem of denial.
c.   Determining what resources, if any, may serve as appropriate referrals.

D.   Following this discussion, summarize your conclusions.

Chapter 7 Competencies/Practice Behaviors Exercises Assessment:

Name: _____ Date: _____

Supervisor's Name: _____

Focus Competencies/Practice Behaviors:
- EP 2.1.1c   Attend to professional roles and boundaries
- EP 2.1.1d   Demonstrate professional demeanor in behavior, appearance, and communication
- EP 2.1.2a   Recognize and manage personal values in a way that allows professional values to guide practice
- EP 2.1.3b   Analyze models of assessment, prevention, intervention, and evaluation
- EP 2.1.3c   Demonstrate effective oral and written communication in working with individuals, families, groups, organizations, communities, and colleagues
- EP 2.1.4b   Gain sufficient self-awareness to eliminate the influence of personal biases and values in working with diverse groups
- EP 2.1.7a   Utilize conceptual frameworks to guide the process of assessment, intervention, and evaluation
- EP 2.1.7b   Critique and apply knowledge to understand person and environment
- EP 2.1.10a   Substantively and affectively prepare for action with individuals, families, groups, organizations, and communities
- EP 2.1.10b   Use empathy and other interpersonal skills
- EP 2.1.10c   Develop a mutually agreed-on focus of work and desired outcomes
- EP 2.1.10d   Collect, organize, and interpret client data
- EP 2.1.10e   Assess client strengths and limitations
- EP 2.1.10f   Develop mutually agreed-on intervention goals and objectives
- EP 2.1.10g   Select appropriate intervention strategies
- EP 2.1.10j   Help clients resolve problems

Instructions:
A.   Evaluate your work or your partner's work in the Focus Competencies/Practice Behaviors by completing the Competencies/Practice Behaviors Assessment form below
B.   What other Competencies/Practice Behaviors did you use to complete these Exercises? Be sure to record them in your assessments

1.	I have attained this competency/practice behavior (in the range of 81 to 100%)
2.	I have largely attained this competency/practice behavior (in the range of 61 to 80%)
3.	I have partially attained this competency/practice behavior (in the range of 41 to 60%)
4.	I have made a little progress in attaining this competency/practice behavior (in the range of 21 to 40%)
5.	I have made almost no progress in attaining this competency/practice behavior (in the range of 0 to 20%)

EPAS 2008 Core Competencies & Core Practice Behaviors	Student Self Assessment						Evaluator Feedback
Student and Evaluator Assessment Scale and Comments	0	1	2	3	4	5	Agree/Disagree/Comments
EP 2.1.1 Identify as a Professional Social Worker and Conduct Oneself Accordingly:							
a. Advocate for client access to the services of social work							
b. Practice personal reflection and self-correction to assure continual professional development							

102

c.	Attend to professional roles and boundaries					
d.	Demonstrate professional demeanor in behavior, appearance, and communication					
e.	Engage in career-long learning					
f.	Use supervision and consultation					
EP 2.1.2 Apply Social Work Ethical Principles to Guide Professional Practice:						
a.	Recognize and manage personal values in a way that allows professional values to guide practice					
b.	Make ethical decisions by applying NASW Code of Ethics and, as applicable, of the IFSW/IASSW Ethics in Social Work, Statement of Principles					
c.	Tolerate ambiguity in resolving ethical conflicts					
d.	Apply strategies of ethical reasoning to arrive at principled decisions					
EP 2.1.3 Apply Critical Thinking to Inform and Communicate Professional Judgments:						
a.	Distinguish, appraise, and integrate multiple sources of knowledge, including research-based knowledge and practice wisdom					
b.	Analyze models of assessment, prevention, intervention, and evaluation					
c.	Demonstrate effective oral and written communication in working with individuals, families, groups, organizations, communities, and colleagues					
EP 2.1.4 Engage Diversity and Difference in Practice:						
a.	Recognize the extent to which a culture's structures and values may oppress, marginalize, alienate, or create or enhance privilege and power					
b.	Gain sufficient self-awareness to eliminate the influence of personal biases and values in working with diverse groups					
c.	Recognize and communicate their understanding of the importance of difference in shaping life experiences					
d.	View themselves as learners and engage those with whom they work as informants					
EP 2.1.5 Advance Human Rights and Social and Economic Justice:						
a.	Understand forms and mechanisms of oppression and discrimination					
b.	Advocate for human rights and social and economic justice					
c.	Engage in practices that advance social and economic justice					
EP 2.1.6 Engage in Research-Informed Practice and Practice-Informed Research:						
a.	Use practice experience to inform scientific inquiry					
b.	Use research evidence to inform practice					

EP 2.1.7 Apply Knowledge of Human Behavior and the Social Environment:						
a.	Utilize conceptual frameworks to guide the processes of assessment, intervention, and evaluation					
b.	Critique and apply knowledge to understand person and environment					
EP 2.1.8 Engage in Policy Practice to Advance Social and Economic Well-Being and to Deliver Effective Social Work Services:						
a.	Analyze, formulate, and advocate for policies that advance social well-being					
b.	Collaborate with colleagues and clients for effective policy action					
EP 2.1.9 Respond to Contexts that Shape Practice:						
a.	Continuously discover, appraise, and attend to changing locales, populations, scientific and technological developments, and emerging societal trends to provide relevant services					
b.	Provide leadership in promoting sustainable changes in service delivery and practice to improve the quality of social services					
EP 2.1.10 Engage, Assess, Intervene, and Evaluate with Individuals, Families, Groups, Organizations and Communities:						
a.	Substantively and affectively prepare for action with individuals, families, groups, organizations, and communities					
b.	Use empathy and other interpersonal skills					
c.	Develop a mutually agreed-on focus of work and desired outcomes					
d.	Collect, organize, and interpret client data					
e.	Assess client strengths and limitations					
f.	Develop mutually agreed-on intervention goals and objectives					
g.	Select appropriate intervention strategies					
h.	Initiate actions to achieve organizational goals					
i.	Implement prevention interventions that enhance client capacities					
j.	Help clients resolve problems					
k.	Negotiate, mediate, and advocate for clients					
l.	Facilitate transitions and endings					
m.	Critically analyze, monitor, and evaluate interventions					

Chapter 8
Evaluation, Termination, and Follow-Up in Generalist Practice

Competencies/Practice Behaviors Exercise 8.1
Key Concepts

Focus Competencies or Practice Behaviors:
- EP 2.1.3   Apply critical thinking to inform and communicate professional judgments
- EP 2.1.7a   Utilize conceptual frameworks to guide the process of assessment, intervention, and evaluation
- EP 2.1.10m   Critically analyze, monitor, and evaluate interventions

Instructions:

A.   Review the section of Chapter 8 entitled Key Terms and Ideas.
B.   Listed below are several statements regarding some of the key concepts described in Chapter 8. Read each of them carefully.
C.   For each statement, use the space provided to answer the questions posed.

Key Concept Statements

a.   Frank says an assertiveness program which has proven successful with six nonassertive clients can be utilized for *all* nonassertive clients. He states the success of one program can be *generalized* to *all* clients with the same problem. Is he right? Why or why not?

_____

_____

_____

b.   A paper-and-pencil questionnaire seems to accurately distinguish between clients who are depressed and those who are not. Clients with a score over 30 on the questionnaire are usually given both anti-depression medication and counseling when they are seen by a psychiatrist. Would this suggest that the questionnaire is a *valid* measure of depression? Why or why not?

_____

_____

_____

c.   Mary and John are arguing about the meaning of *dependent* and *independent variables*. John says that the interventions he is doing with a family constitute the *dependent variable* and the changes the parents have made, such as praising the children more and communicating feelings to one another, are the *independent variables*. Mary says John has the concepts backward. Who is right and why?

_____

_____

_____

---

d.	Alice has been using an at-home pregnancy test to determine if she is pregnant. The test has given different results on three occasions. Alice says the test does not seem *reliable*. Is she right? Why or why not?

_____

_____

_____

e.	At the conclusion of each group session, Ed, the social worker, asks the group members to give their opinions about how well the group functioned during the session. Ed commented to a colleague that he does this as one type of *formative evaluation*. Has Ed correctly described this type of evaluation?

_____

_____

_____

Competencies/Practice Behaviors Exercise 8.2
Alternative Outcome Explanations

Focus Competencies or Practice Behaviors:
- EP 2.1.3	Apply critical thinking to inform and communicate professional judgments
- EP 2.1.7a	Utilize conceptual frameworks to guide the process of assessment, intervention, and evaluation
- EP 2.1.10m	Critically analyze, monitor, and evaluate interventions

Instructions:
A.	Read each of the following case situations.
B.	Select an alternative explanation for the outcome which seems most probable given your knowledge of evaluation.

Case Situation #1
A group for twelve delinquent adolescents was begun ten weeks ago by the Juvenile Probation Department. The group was voluntary and involved regular sessions with a probation officer who asked the members to talk about their feelings. Six of the members dropped out along the way. Each of the six that remained evaluated the group experience very positively. Which of the following explanations might better explain the "successful" outcome.
a.	History
b.	Maturation
c.	Mortality
d.	Reactance
What is the reason for your answer?

Case Situation #2

Five very nonassertive adults joined a group to teach them to be more assertive. The group met for twelve weeks. Each person in the group was given an assertiveness test before joining and during the twelfth session. All showed more assertiveness on the last test. Other than an effective assertiveness training program, what might account for the change in their scores from the first session to the last?

a.   Maturation
b.   Regression toward the mean
c.   Mortality
d.   Creaming

What is the reason for your answer?

Case Situation #3

You see an advertisement for a new program which claims a high rate of success in treating anorexia (an eating disorder). The only people admitted to the program are those who have been through a battery of tests and interviews. All candidates are evaluated on their motivation to change, and only those with the highest motivation are admitted to the program. What might explain the very positive outcomes claimed by this program?

a.   Maturation
b.   History
c.   Mortality
d.   Creaming

What is the reason for your answer?

Competencies/Practice Behaviors Exercise 8.3
Addressing Feelings About Termination

Focus Competencies or Practice Behaviors:
- EP 2.1.3   Apply critical thinking to inform and communicate professional judgments
- EP 2.1.10l   Facilitate transitions and endings

Instructions:
A.   Read each of the following excerpts from a worker-client interview.
B.   For each vignette, select one worker response which appears to be the most appropriate and circle your choice.
C.   Compare your answers with the class.

107

Vignette #1

Joan is meeting the worker for the last time. She appears a bit red-eyed near the end of the session as they finish their discussion about how much has happened in the past six months. Ann, the worker, is unsure of what might be going on in Joan's mind since they have talked about termination at previous meetings. Which of the following might be an appropriate response on Ann's part?

a.   Let's not get too choked up now; you are doing fine.

b.   You seem a little teary just now. What are you feeling?

c.   You seem upset. Should we meet once more to talk about how things are going?

Vignette #2

Jan has just gotten a new job as a nurse's aide. She seems happy and expresses her glee to her social worker, Dorothy, at their last session together. What should Dorothy say?

a.   I am so happy for you and delighted that you have found something that really interests you. You really look excited.

b.   You are happy now but I worry about how you will get along after our sessions are over. This has been an important part of your life and I would think you might miss it. Many others have.

c.   Let's talk about how you're feeling about the ending of our relationship. I feel a bit blue that we won't be seeing each other every week.

Vignette #3

Susan appears distraught and anxious at the beginning of the next-to-the-last session. She states that she really does not feel that she has made much progress in her work with Mark, and wonders aloud whether this has all been a waste of time. Now Mark is confused. What might he say?

a.   You seem pretty upset today. I wonder what's going on.

b.   We have accomplished a great deal together and I wonder how you can say we haven't made much progress.

c.   Susan, something is troubling you today. I sense that you may be reacting to the ending of our sessions. A common reaction to termination is to be fearful of the future. People often question whether they've accomplished anything. Perhaps you are a bit angry with me. Do any of these strike a chord with you?

Competencies/Practice Behaviors Exercise 8.4
Role-Play: Evaluation of Practice

Focus Competencies or Practice Behaviors:
- EP 2.1.3   Apply critical thinking to inform and communicate professional judgments
- EP 2.1.10m   Critically analyze, monitor, and evaluate interventions

Instructions:

A.   Review the four evaluation designs for generalist practice discussed in the text. They are single-subject designs, task-achievement and goal-attainment scaling, and client satisfaction questionnaires. Also review the five types of evaluation designs for programs (needs assessments, evaluability assessments, process analysis, program outcome analysis, and program monitoring).

B.   The instructor will assign students to task groups of four to six people. Each group will participate in a role play. Identify one person to serve as recorder for each group.

C. Below is a case situation describing the need for evaluation within a social agency. Read the case carefully.

Case Situation: The Morningside Center

Marian Edwards is the coordinator of juvenile services for the Morningside Center, a small private agency that has a contract with the Department of Human Services. Under the terms of the contract, the Morningside Center provides after-school recreational and group activities for adolescent males and females. The Department of Human Services is requiring an evaluation component in all future contracts, and the Morningside Center's contract is up for renewal. Marian has been asked to design an evaluation mechanism that will help determine whether Morningside Center is achieving its purpose of giving adolescents a place to go so that they can stay out of trouble. Many of the adolescents in the Morningside area are at-risk for involvement in delinquent behavior. It is this behavior that the Department of Human Services is most interested in preventing. Marian is meeting with her staff to discuss the need to design an evaluation program. You are part of that staff for purposes of this exercise.

D. Assess the four evaluation designs to establish which one seems appropriate for use in this situation. Use the following format for your assessment:

Design	Pros	Cons
Single-subject design:		
Goal-attainment scaling:		
Task-achievement scaling:		
Client satisfaction questionnaire:		

1. Select the design that seems most appropriate to this situation and list three reasons why this design is best.

    a.   Most appropriate design: _____

    b.   Reasons why this design is best:
        1) _____
        2) _____
        3) _____

2. Identify at least two types of information that might be gathered for use in this evaluation. Identify the sources or methods by which this information might be acquired.

    a.   Types of information:
        1) _____
        2) _____
        3) _____

    b.   Methods for gathering information:
        1) _____
        2) _____

3. Assume that the evaluation design you select has been in use for two years. Of the five types of evaluation designs for programs mentioned in the text (needs assessments, evaluability assessments, process analysis, program outcome analysis, and program monitoring), which is best suited to the task of determining whether the Morningside Center is effective?

_____
_____

Why is it the most suited?

_____
_____

E.   Record your responses and report them back to the larger class at the direction of the instructor.

F.   Your instructor will lead a class discussion focusing on the following questions:

1. Why do social workers seem more interested in "doing" social work than in "evaluating" it?

110

2. Why is evaluation of social work practice important? To whom is it important?

3. Does a funding body such as the Department of Human Services have a right to require an evaluation component in contracts they sign with other agencies? Why or why not?

Chapter 8 Competencies/Practice Behaviors Exercises Assessment:

Name: _____ **Date:** _____

Supervisor's Name: _____

Focus Competencies/Practice Behaviors:
- EP 2.1.3   Apply critical thinking to inform and communicate professional judgments
- EP 2.1.7a   Utilize conceptual frameworks to guide the process of assessment, intervention, and evaluation
- EP 2.1.10l   Facilitate transitions and endings
- EP 2.1.10m   Critically analyze, monitor, and evaluate interventions

Instructions:
A.   Evaluate your work or your partner's work in the Focus Competencies/Practice Behaviors by completing the Competencies/Practice Behaviors Assessment form below
B.   What other Competencies/Practice Behaviors did you use to complete these Exercises? Be sure to record them in your assessments

1.	I have attained this competency/practice behavior (in the range of 81 to 100%)
2.	I have largely attained this competency/practice behavior (in the range of 61 to 80%)
3.	I have partially attained this competency/practice behavior (in the range of 41 to 60%)
4.	I have made a little progress in attaining this competency/practice behavior (in the range of 21 to 40%)
5.	I have made almost no progress in attaining this competency/practice behavior (in the range of 0 to 20%)

EPAS 2008 Core Competencies & Core Practice Behaviors	Student Self Assessment						Evaluator Feedback
Student and Evaluator Assessment Scale and Comments	0	1	2	3	4	5	**Agree/Disagree/Comments**
EP 2.1.1 Identify as a Professional Social Worker and Conduct Oneself Accordingly:							
a. Advocate for client access to the services of social work							
b. Practice personal reflection and self-correction to assure continual professional development							
c. Attend to professional roles and boundaries							
d. Demonstrate professional demeanor in behavior, appearance, and communication							
e. Engage in career-long learning							
f. Use supervision and consultation							
EP 2.1.2 Apply Social Work Ethical Principles to Guide Professional Practice:							
a. Recognize and manage personal values in a way that allows professional values to guide practice							
b. Make ethical decisions by applying NASW Code of Ethics and, as applicable, of the IFSW/IASSW Ethics in Social Work, Statement of Principles							
c. Tolerate ambiguity in resolving ethical conflicts							
d. Apply strategies of ethical reasoning to arrive at principled decisions							

112

EP 2.1.3 Apply Critical Thinking to Inform and Communicate Professional Judgments:							
a.	Distinguish, appraise, and integrate multiple sources of knowledge, including research-based knowledge and practice wisdom						
b.	Analyze models of assessment, prevention, intervention, and evaluation						
c.	Demonstrate effective oral and written communication in working with individuals, families, groups, organizations, communities, and colleagues						
EP 2.1.4 Engage Diversity and Difference in Practice:							
a.	Recognize the extent to which a culture's structures and values may oppress, marginalize, alienate, or create or enhance privilege and power						
b.	Gain sufficient self-awareness to eliminate the influence of personal biases and values in working with diverse groups						
c.	Recognize and communicate their understanding of the importance of difference in shaping life experiences						
d.	View themselves as learners and engage those with whom they work as informants						
EP 2.1.5 Advance Human Rights and Social and Economic Justice:							
a.	Understand forms and mechanisms of oppression and discrimination						
b.	Advocate for human rights and social and economic justice						
c.	Engage in practices that advance social and economic justice						
EP 2.1.6 Engage in Research-Informed Practice and Practice-Informed Research:							
a.	Use practice experience to inform scientific inquiry						
b.	Use research evidence to inform practice						
EP 2.1.7 Apply Knowledge of Human Behavior and the Social Environment:							
a.	Utilize conceptual frameworks to guide the processes of assessment, intervention, and evaluation						
b.	Critique and apply knowledge to understand person and environment						
EP 2.1.8 Engage in Policy Practice to Advance Social and Economic Well-Being and to Deliver Effective Social Work Services:							
a.	Analyze, formulate, and advocate for policies that advance social well-being						
b.	Collaborate with colleagues and clients for effective policy action						
EP 2.1.9 Respond to Contexts that Shape Practice:							
a.	Continuously discover, appraise, and attend to changing locales, populations, scientific and technological developments, and emerging societal trends to provide relevant services						
b.	Provide leadership in promoting sustainable changes in service delivery and practice to improve the quality of social services						

113

EP 2.1.10 Engage, Assess, Intervene, and Evaluate with Individuals, Families, Groups, Organizations and Communities:							
a.	Substantively and affectively prepare for action with individuals, families, groups, organizations, and communities						
b.	Use empathy and other interpersonal skills						
c.	Develop a mutually agreed-on focus of work and desired outcomes						
d.	Collect, organize, and interpret client data						
e.	Assess client strengths and limitations						
f.	Develop mutually agreed-on intervention goals and objectives						
g.	Select appropriate intervention strategies						
h.	Initiate actions to achieve organizational goals						
i.	Implement prevention interventions that enhance client capacities						
j.	Help clients resolve problems						
k.	Negotiate, mediate, and advocate for clients						
l.	Facilitate transitions and endings						
m.	Critically analyze, monitor, and evaluate interventions						

Competencies/Practice Behaviors Exercise 9.1
Family Roles

Focus Competencies or Practice Behaviors:
- EP 2.1.1b   Practice personal reflection and self-correction to assure continual professional development
- EP 2.1.7b   Critique and apply knowledge to understand person and environment
- EP 2.1.10a   Substantively and affectively prepare for action with individuals, families, groups, organizations, and communities

Instructions:
A.   Prior to the exercise, review the material in the text on family assessment skills, especially that concerning family roles.
B.   Focus either on your family of origin or on your current family configuration. Take about ten minutes to write down answers to the questions below about family roles.[1]

Family Roles

a.   What specific roles does each family member occupy?

_____
_____
_____
_____

b.   Do the various roles played work well together for the family's benefit?

_____
_____
_____
_____

c.   Are any of the roles ambiguous, redundant, or left empty? Please explain.

_____
_____
_____
_____

d.   Is there flexibility among family roles so that the family is better able to adjust to crisis situations? Please explain.

_____
_____
_____
_____

---

[1] These questions are used when assessing families. See A.M. Holman, *Family Assessment: Tools for Understanding and Intervention* (Beverly Hills, CA: Sage, 1983), p. 30.

e. Do the family's roles conform with basic social norms? (For example, society does not condone a criminal role.)

_____
_____
_____
_____

f. Do the family's roles function to enhance the family's feelings of self-worth and well-being or detract from these feelings? Please explain.

_____
_____
_____
_____
_____

C. Answer the following questions:

1. What roles are most pronounced in your family?

2. What value judgments did you find yourself making about your family's roles?

3. What roles do you think are most pronounced in families generally?

4. What roles do you think emphasize the uniqueness of your family?

116

5.   Can you think of a dysfunctional family you know?

6.   What, if any, problems regarding roles did the family members experience?

7.   What types of role problems do you think you will be most likely to confront in practice?

Competencies/Practice Behaviors Exercise 9.2
Family Resources

Focus Competencies or Practice Behaviors:
- EP 2.1.7b   Critique and apply knowledge to understand person and environment
- EP 2.1.10d   Collect, organize, and interpret client data
- EP 2.1.10e   Assess client strengths and limitations

Instructions:
A.   Before beginning the exercise, review the information provided in the text concerning assessing a family's access to resources.

B.   Take about 10 minutes to fill out the form presented below, which is the first section of "Family Access to Basic Resources (FABR)."[2] Before beginning, establish the boundaries of your family. Focus on your current family, your family of origin, or yourself if you are single. It doesn't matter which family group you decide is appropriate. The important thing is to have a specific family group in mind.

---

[2] Reprinted from Nancy R. Vosler, "Assessing Family Access to Basic Resources: An Essential Component of Social Work Practice," in *Social Work*, 35(5) (1990), pp. 436-37. Reprinted with permission of the author and of the National Association of Social Workers, Silver Spring, MD.

Family Access to Basic Resources (FABR)

Part 1—Monthly expenses for a family of this size and composition

Work expenses
  Transportation: $___
  Child care: ___
  Taxes: ___
Purchases for basic needs
  Decent housing: ___
  Utilities: ___
  Food: ___
  Clothing: ___
  Personal care: ___
  Recreation: ___

Health care
  Medical: ___
  Dental: ___
  Mental health: ___
  Special (e.g., substance abuse):   ___
  Education: ___
  Family & developmental
    (counseling) services: ___
Procurement of resources/
  services (e.g., transportation):   ___

  Monthly Total: $___

Part 2—Potential monthly family resources

Money income
    Wages (if parents' occupations are known, what are average
      monthly wages for these types of jobs?): $___
    Child support (if applicable):   ___
    Income transfers (for those unemployed or not expected to work)
      Unemployment insurance: ___
      Worker's compensation: ___
      Social Security: ___
      Supplemental Security Income (SSI):   ___
      Aid to Families with Dependent Children (AFDC)[3]:   ___
      Other (e.g., general relief, emergency assistance):   ___
Credits, goods, and services (free or sliding scale):
    Housing
      Section 8:   ___
      Other housing assistance (e.g., public housing,
        shelter, hotel/motel):   ___
      Utilities assistance: ___

---

[3] AFDC was "a public assistance program . . . funded by the federal and state governments to provide financial aid for needy children who are deprived of parental support because of death, incapacitation, or absence" (Barker, 1999, p. 15). The Personal Responsibility Act (PRA) passed by Congress in August, 1996, abolished AFDC "which had provided support for poor children and their mothers since its inception at Title IV of the 1935 Social Security Act;" AFDC was replaced by "block grants for Temporary Assistance to Needy Families (TANF) which "put a cap on federal funds provided to the states" and allowed states greater discretion in benefit distribution (Abramovitz, 1997, pp. 311-312). The purpose of the FABR questionnaire is to determine resources regardless of their source. Therefore, you might replace the AFDC category with other new programs providing benefits to children and families.

Food
        Food stamps: ___
        Women's, Infants', and Children's Supplementary
                Food Program (WIC):   ___
        Food bank, food pantry, and other food assistance: ___

                                      Monthly Total: $___

Clothing: Access to used clothing store?   Yes ☐ No ☐
Personal care and recreation:
        Access to free recreational facilities?   Yes ☐ No ☐
Health care
        Medicare?   Yes ☐ No ☐
        Medicaid?   Yes ☐ No ☐
        Health clinic?   Yes ☐ No ☐
        Dental clinic?   Yes ☐ No ☐
        Mental health services?   Yes ☐ No ☐
        Special services (e.g., drug abuse treatment)?   Yes ☐ No ☐
Education
        Public education?   Yes ☐ No ☐
        Special education?   Yes ☐ No ☐
        Tutoring?   Yes ☐ No ☐
        General Equivalency Diploma (GED)?   Yes ☐ No ☐
        Job Training?   Yes ☐ No ☐
Family and developmental (counseling) services
        Family services?   Yes ☐ No ☐
        Support groups?   Yes ☐ No ☐
        Family life education?   Yes ☐ No ☐
Procurement
        Transportation?   Yes ☐ No ☐

Part 3—Current Resources

Access to resources last month

Money income

Wages (use net pay; then subtract	Clothing: $___
other work expenses from Part I	Personal care and health care: ___
including child care, transpor-	Education: ___
tation, etc.): $___	Family & developmental
Child Support: ___	services: ___
Income transfers: ___	Procurement: ___
Credits, goods, & services:	
Housing: ___	
Food: ___	Monthly Total: ___

C.   Answer the following questions:

1.   How did it feel to fill out the FABR?

2.   To what extent was it uncomfortable to share such personal information?

3.   To what extent could you remember all of the detailed information requested?

4.   Were there resources mentioned on the form that you didn't know about or didn't understand? If so, which ones and why?

5.   How useful do you think the FABR might be in real worker/client practice situations?

6.   What did you learn from this experience?

Focus Competencies or Practice Behaviors:

- EP 2.1.3a   Distinguish, appraise, and integrate multiple sources of knowledge, including research-based knowledge and practice wisdom
- EP 2.1.8a   Analyze, formulate, and advocate for policies that advance social well-being
- EP 2.1.9a   Continuously discover, appraise, and attend to changing locales, populations, scientific and technological developments, and emerging societal trends to provide relevant services

Instructions:

A.   Read the questions below and record your answers.

Policy Areas Impacting Families

1.   Employment

   a.   What policies do you think would increase employment and decrease unemployment?

   b.   Should government subsidize industry in order to hire new workers or prevent laying off current workers?

   c.   Should taxes be levied on foreign imports?

   d.   Should the government expand old and set up new job training programs?

   e.   What would the costs of such policies be?

f.   What can you do to help your clients gain adequate employment under such circumstances if few or no programs and policies exist to help you?

2.   *Direct provision of income or substitutes for income*

   a.   What do you do when your clients aren't eligible for enough cash and in-kind (for example, food stamps) income transfers to survive?

   b.   What do you do if policies neglect clients who are slowly starving to death?

3.   *Health care* (Millions of poor underemployed and unemployed people in this country are not covered.)

   a.   What health care policies should this country adopt to cover your clients who are poor and not currently covered?

   b.   Who should pay for such programs?

4.   *Homeless people*

   a.   What can you as a social worker do if there are no programs with policies to provide your clients temporary shelter, food, and longer-term housing?

b.   What can you do if families are living literally on the streets?

5.   *Day care* (Most women work. More specifically, most women with children work. Adequate day care for their children is often difficult to find. It's also expensive and the quality is highly variable.)

    a.   Should the federal, state, and/or local governments establish policies to provide resources for day care so that parents can work?

    b.   Are you and others willing to pay taxes to finance these services?

    c.   What if your client is a single parent who receives public assistance payments barely allowing her to subsist below the poverty level? When benefits cease and she is forced to seek employment outside of the home, what if she can't afford the available day care? What policy changes might help her?

6.   *Child support maintenance* (Policies dictate how much support divorced fathers provide their children. [Of course, mothers may also be required to provide support to children living with their fathers; however, this occurs infrequently.] Policies also mandate how the receipt of that support is monitored.)

    a.   What if your single-parent, female client is not receiving the child support payments she needs to survive?

123

b.   Do existing policies indicate that a portion of the father's salary can be garnisheed, that is, legally removed from his pay and sent to his family before he receives his paycheck?

c.   Will policies mandate that this happens automatically, or must the mother seek legal counsel to advocate for her?

d.   What happens if the father moves to another state?

e.   Will that state's policies allow the garnishment of wages?

f.   What if your client, a single parent and mother of two, works for a minimum wage, can't afford adequate housing on that income, and desperately needs support payments to subsist?

Competencies/Practice Behaviors Exercise 9.4
Role-Play: Clarifying Family Resources

Focus Competencies or Practice Behaviors:
- EP 2.1.7b   Critique and apply knowledge to understand person and environment
- EP 2.1.10a   Substantively and affectively prepare for action with individuals, families, groups, organizations, and communities
- EP 2.1.10d   Collect, organize, and interpret client data
- EP 2.1.10e   Assess client strengths and limitations

Instructions:

A.   Before beginning the exercise, review the information provided in the text concerning assessing a family's access to resources.

B.   Complete Exercise 2 above.

C.   Divide into pairs. Arbitrarily determine who will be the "worker" (that is, the person who will do the assessment) and who will be the "client" (that is, the person providing information).

D.   The worker should take about twenty minutes to complete the portion of the Family Access to Basic Resources (FABR) questionnaire provided below. This involves clarifying some of the information already gathered in Exercise 2.

Resource Stability[4]

How stable was each resource over the past year (very stable, somewhat stable, somewhat unstable, very unstable)? Discuss for each type of resource.

Wages: Overall access to wages through employment? Types of jobs available? Part-time or full-time? Wage levels? Benefits? How would/do you deal with child care or supervision of youth? Quality of child care? Do you have choices? How would/do you deal with an ill child? How would/do you get to and from work? What education and training are needed for good jobs? What education and training opportunities are available? Have you been laid off or terminated or experienced a plant closing? Number of times unemployed? Length of time unemployed?

Housing: Rent or own? Choice? Maintenance a problem? Are utilities adequate? Have you been put on a waiting list or been dropped from Section 8 or other housing assistance? Have you had to move or been evicted because the landlord converted to higher rents, condominiums, etc.? Have you experienced homelessness?

Clothing: Variety for different roles?

Personal care and recreation: What kinds of recreation? Individual? Family?

Health Care: High quality? Choice? Available in a crisis? Have you been dropped from health care coverage with an employer or from Medicaid? If so, why? Have you or another family member been put on a waiting list, for example, for medical or dental care, for counseling for a mental health problem, or for treatment for alcohol or drug abuse? If so, how long did the person have to wait for services?

Other comments and reflections:

---

[4] Reprinted from Nancy R. Vosler, "Assessing Family Access to Basic Resources: An Essential Component of Social Work Practice," in *Social Work* 35(5) (1990), pp. 436-37. Reprinted with permission of the author and of the National Association of Social Workers, Silver Spring, MD.

E.   Rejoin the class for a ten minute discussion and then answer the following questions and issues:

   1.   For the worker, how difficult was it to clarify the resources?

   2.   What areas, if any, did you have difficulty understanding?

   3.   Did you find yourself making value judgments in any areas?

   4.   For the client, how did it feel to participate in the interview process?

   5.   What information, if any, did you feel the worker misunderstood or missed?

   6.   How useful do you feel such a resource assessment instrument would be in real practice situations? Why or why not?

   7.   To what extent do you feel such an instrument might give you clues to undertaking macro and mezzo interventions? What are your reasons?

Competencies/Practice Behaviors Exercise 9.5
Role-Play: Problem Solving with Couples

Focus Competencies or Practice Behaviors:
- EP 2.1.1c   Attend to professional roles and boundaries
- EP 2.1.3c   Demonstrate effective oral and written communication in working with individuals, families, groups, organizations, communities, and colleagues
- EP 2.1.10a   Substantively and affectively prepare for action with individuals, families, groups, organizations, and communities
- EP 2.1.10b   Use empathy and other interpersonal skills
- EP 2.1.10c   Develop a mutually agreed-on focus of work and desired outcomes
- EP 2.1.10d   Collect, organize, and interpret client data
- EP 2.1.10e   Assess client strengths and limitations
- EP 2.1.10f   Develop mutually agreed-on intervention goals and objectives
- EP 2.1.10g   Select appropriate intervention strategies
- EP 2.1.10j   Help clients resolve problems

Instructions:
A.   Review the material in the text on family assessment skills and family conflicts.
B.   Volunteers are needed to assume the following roles:

Role Play: Problem Solving with Couples

Social Work Role:
Two social workers do intake and provide some problem-solving counseling for Oshkosh County Social Services Department. The county is primarily rural so the workers assess a wide range of problems, provide help, and make referrals where appropriate.

Client Role:
Fred, twenty-seven, is a pleasantly attractive, slender person with an outgoing, likable personality. He works second shift in a donut factory, and has an annual salary of $22,000.

Client Role:
Ethel, twenty-five, is a nervous, intense person who frequently has a worried expression on her face. She refers to herself as being "very shy." She has a pretty face and is about twenty-five pounds overweight. Since before her marriage she has worked as a secretary for an Internet company. She earns approximately $23,000 annually. She also appears basically likable and eager to please.

The Presenting Problem:
Fred and Ethel have been married for four years. They come to Social Services because they are experiencing "marital problems."
   Fred says that the problem is that he and Ethel fight all the time when they're together. He says he loves his wife and is committed to making his marriage work. He does not believe in divorce for moral and religious reasons. He and Ethel both want to have a family in a few years. He says Ethel always nags him about going out for a few beers after work with the boys and about how he really doesn't love her. No matter how much he tells her he loves her, she doesn't seem to believe him.

127

Ethel says the problem is that Fred ignores her all the time. He doesn't seem very interested in talking to her or spending time with her. She says she loves him very much and is committed to making the marriage work. She does not believe in divorce for moral and religious reasons. She and Fred both want to have a family in a few years. Ethel says she's getting more and more depressed about their marital situation and lack of communication. She constantly criticizes herself and wonders what she's doing wrong.

C. Fred and Ethel also have hidden agendas which are recorded at the end of this chapter's exercise section. *Do not look at them at this time.* Only Fred and Ethel should read them before the role play. One intent of this exercise is for the workers to seek out information and identify problems. The hidden agendas will be shared later after the role play.

D. The role play will begin in the middle of the interview. It is assumed that the workers have already gathered the information cited above. Their task now is to complete their assessment, prioritize problems, and make referrals as appropriate.

E. During the role play, observers should take notes as they address the following questions:

Feedback Form

1. What do you think are particularly *good techniques* used by the social workers? How did the *clients react* to these techniques? (Please be specific.)

2. Do you see any weaknesses or areas in which improvement would be helpful? (Specific suggestions for how to improve are beneficial.)

3. Do you have any additional thoughts or comments?

F. The role players should sit in the front of the room where other students can clearly observe them. The role play should last no longer than thirty minutes.

G. After thirty minutes, your instructor will stop the role play and read Fred and Ethel's hidden agendas described at the end of this chapter's Exercise section.

H. The class will then participate in a discussion addressing the following issues and questions:

128

1. What feedback did you note on your forms? Strengths? Weaknesses? Other comments?

2. How much of the clients' hidden agendas surfaced during the interview?

3. To what extent were the issues and future plans clear by the end of the interview?

4. To what extent do you think this role play might relate to the issues of real client couples?

5. What did you learn from participating in or observing this role play?

HIDDEN AGENDAS FOR EXERCISE 5 (ONLY FRED AND ETHEL READ THIS)

Fred's Hidden Agenda

Fred has very high expectations for himself concerning being a good provider and husband. He gets very threatened both when Ethel criticizes him and when he feels that he's losing control of his marriage.

Fred's also afraid that Ethel's secretly drinking too much. Sometimes he smells liquor on her breath. Sometimes he finds her passed out. He's also found empty liquor bottles in the garbage. He hasn't said anything about this to her. He's afraid to confront her with it because he thinks it will move them closer to a divorce.

At this point, Fred doesn't know what to do, so he has withdrawn from Ethel. He tries to be pleasant to her but really doesn't talk to her very much. Sometimes to avoid her he goes out for a beer after work with his male friends at the factory.

Ethel's Hidden Agenda

Ethel is a very insecure person with a fairly poor self-concept. She is an expert on what is wrong with herself and sometimes wonders what Fred really sees in her. Her weight also bothers her. Sometimes she just can't stand it anymore and withdraws into drinking. She knows this is wrong and feels very guilty about it. She's drinking just about every day now. She doesn't want Fred to find out and doesn't want to talk about it.

Ethel's really afraid that Fred is turning to other women. There are several attractive women at the donut factory that she's met at parties and that Fred has casually mentioned in the past. She's terrified of losing Fred. Fred works six second-shift days a week and goes out almost every night "with the boys." Ethel thinks he's secretly having an affair. This hurts Ethel terribly. However, she is following her typical pattern of avoidance and has avoided mentioning this to Fred. Frustration has built up and she finds herself nagging and yelling at him a lot for little things.

Chapter 9 Competencies/Practice Behaviors Exercises Assessment:

Name: _____ **Date:** _____

Supervisor's Name: _____

Focus Competencies/Practice Behaviors:

- EP 2.1.1b   Practice personal reflection and self-correction to assure continual professional development
- EP 2.1.1c   Attend to professional roles and boundaries
- EP 2.1.1d   Demonstrate professional demeanor in behavior, appearance, and communication
- EP 2.1.3a   Distinguish, appraise, and integrate multiple sources of knowledge, including research-based knowledge and practice wisdom
- EP 2.1.3c   Demonstrate effective oral and written communication in working with individuals, families, groups, organizations, communities, and colleagues
- EP 2.1.7b   Critique and apply knowledge to understand person and environment
- EP 2.1.8a   Analyze, formulate, and advocate for policies that advance social well-being
- EP 2.1.9a   Continuously discover, appraise, and attend to changing locales, populations, scientific and technological developments, and emerging societal trends to provide relevant services
- EP 2.1.10a   Substantively and affectively prepare for action with individuals, families, groups, organizations, and communities
- EP 2.1.10b   Use empathy and other interpersonal skills
- EP 2.1.10c   Develop a mutually agreed-on focus of work and desired outcomes
- EP 2.1.10d   Collect, organize, and interpret client data
- EP 2.1.10e   Assess client strengths and limitations
- EP 2.1.10f   Develop mutually agreed-on intervention goals and objectives
- EP 2.1.10g   Select appropriate intervention strategies
- EP 2.1.10j   Help clients resolve problems

Instructions:

A.   Evaluate your work or your partner's work in the Focus Competencies/Practice Behaviors by completing the Competencies/Practice Behaviors Assessment form below

B.   What other Competencies/Practice Behaviors did you use to complete these Exercises? Be sure to record them in your assessments

1.	I have attained this competency/practice behavior (in the range of 81 to 100%)
2.	I have largely attained this competency/practice behavior (in the range of 61 to 80%)
3.	I have partially attained this competency/practice behavior (in the range of 41 to 60%)
4.	I have made a little progress in attaining this competency/practice behavior (in the range of 21 to 40%)
5.	I have made almost no progress in attaining this competency/practice behavior (in the range of 0 to 20%)

EPAS 2008 Core Competencies & Core Practice Behaviors							Student Self Assessment	Evaluator Feedback
Student and Evaluator Assessment Scale and Comments	0	1	2	3	4	5		**Agree/Disagree/Comments**
EP 2.1.1 Identify as a Professional Social Worker and Conduct Oneself Accordingly:								
a. Advocate for client access to the services of social work								
b. Practice personal reflection and self-correction to assure continual professional development								

131

c.	Attend to professional roles and boundaries						
d.	Demonstrate professional demeanor in behavior, appearance, and communication						
e.	Engage in career-long learning						
f.	Use supervision and consultation						
EP 2.1.2 Apply Social Work Ethical Principles to Guide Professional Practice:							
a.	Recognize and manage personal values in a way that allows professional values to guide practice						
b.	Make ethical decisions by applying NASW Code of Ethics and, as applicable, of the IFSW/IASSW Ethics in Social Work, Statement of Principles						
c.	Tolerate ambiguity in resolving ethical conflicts						
d.	Apply strategies of ethical reasoning to arrive at principled decisions						
EP 2.1.3 Apply Critical Thinking to Inform and Communicate Professional Judgments:							
a.	Distinguish, appraise, and integrate multiple sources of knowledge, including research-based knowledge and practice wisdom						
b.	Analyze models of assessment, prevention, intervention, and evaluation						
c.	Demonstrate effective oral and written communication in working with individuals, families, groups, organizations, communities, and colleagues						
EP 2.1.4 Engage Diversity and Difference in Practice:							
a.	Recognize the extent to which a culture's structures and values may oppress, marginalize, alienate, or create or enhance privilege and power						
b.	Gain sufficient self-awareness to eliminate the influence of personal biases and values in working with diverse groups						
c.	Recognize and communicate their understanding of the importance of difference in shaping life experiences						
d.	View themselves as learners and engage those with whom they work as informants						
EP 2.1.5 Advance Human Rights and Social and Economic Justice:							
a.	Understand forms and mechanisms of oppression and discrimination						
b.	Advocate for human rights and social and economic justice						
c.	Engage in practices that advance social and economic justice						
EP 2.1.6 Engage in Research-Informed Practice and Practice-Informed Research:							
a.	Use practice experience to inform scientific inquiry						
b.	Use research evidence to inform practice						

132

EP 2.1.7 Apply Knowledge of Human Behavior and the Social Environment:						
a. Utilize conceptual frameworks to guide the processes of assessment, intervention, and evaluation						
b. Critique and apply knowledge to understand person and environment						
EP 2.1.8 Engage in Policy Practice to Advance Social and Economic Well-Being and to Deliver Effective Social Work Services:						
a. Analyze, formulate, and advocate for policies that advance social well-being						
b. Collaborate with colleagues and clients for effective policy action						
EP 2.1.9 Respond to Contexts that Shape Practice:						
a. Continuously discover, appraise, and attend to changing locales, populations, scientific and technological developments, and emerging societal trends to provide relevant services						
b. Provide leadership in promoting sustainable changes in service delivery and practice to improve the quality of social services						
EP 2.1.10 Engage, Assess, Intervene, and Evaluate with Individuals, Families, Groups, Organizations and Communities:						
a. Substantively and affectively prepare for action with individuals, families, groups, organizations, and communities						
b. Use empathy and other interpersonal skills						
c. Develop a mutually agreed-on focus of work and desired outcomes						
d. Collect, organize, and interpret client data						
e. Assess client strengths and limitations						
f. Develop mutually agreed-on intervention goals and objectives						
g. Select appropriate intervention strategies						
h. Initiate actions to achieve organizational goals						
i. Implement prevention interventions that enhance client capacities						
j. Help clients resolve problems						
k. Negotiate, mediate, and advocate for clients						
l. Facilitate transitions and endings						
m. Critically analyze, monitor, and evaluate interventions						

133

Competencies/Practice Behaviors Exercise 10.1
Role-Play: Beginnings with Families

Focus Competencies or Practice Behaviors:

- EP 2.1.1c   Attend to professional roles and boundaries
- EP 2.1.1d   Demonstrate professional demeanor in behavior, appearance, and communication
- EP 2.1.3c   Demonstrate effective oral and written communication in working with individuals, families, groups, organizations, communities, and colleagues
- EP 2.1.10a   Substantively and affectively prepare for action with individuals, families, groups, organizations, and communities
- EP 2.1.10b   Use empathy and other interpersonal skills
- EP 2.1.10c   Develop a mutually agreed-on focus of work and desired outcomes
- EP 2.1.10d   Collect, organize, and interpret client data
- EP 2.1.10e   Assess client strengths and limitations
- EP 2.1.10f   Develop mutually agreed-on intervention goals and objectives
- EP 2.1.10g   Select appropriate intervention strategies
- EP 2.1.10j   Help clients resolve problems

Instructions:

A.   Before beginning the exercise, review the material in the text on beginnings with families. It emphasizes information that will be the focus of the exercise.[1] Initial goals include:

        a.   Get a clear picture of the problem.
        b.   Gain the family's consent to treatment.
        c.   Set procedures for change in motion.

The five phases for beginning treatment include:

        a.   Alleviate or at least minimize early apprehension.
        b.   Ask family members to explain what's wrong.
        c.   Establish agreement about what's wrong.
        d.   Concentrate on how family members relate to each other.
        e.   Establish commitment to a plan of action.

B.   Read the role-play described below. Volunteers are needed for each role. Otherwise, your instructor will assign roles.

---

[1] The initial goals and five phases presented here are primarily based on material found in *Family Treatment in Social Work Practice* (4th ed.) by C. Janzen and O. Harris (Itasca, IL: F.E. Peacock, 2006).

Role Play: A Nontraditional Family

Social Work Role:

The social workers are counselors at a family services clinic. They accept call-in referrals and provide short-term counseling, emphasizing problem solving, primarily to families. On occasion, they provide individual counseling to family members in order to work on specific issues or problems.

The Situation:

This is the first interview with June Cleaver, her daughter, Waleeta, sixteen, and son, Beaver, eleven. June and her ex-husband Ward have just completed the divorce process. June called the agency in panic because of pain and confusion resulting from the divorce. You received the information presented below from the intake worker's report.

Client Role:

June, thirty-eight, is a mild-mannered, friendly, responsive, attractive woman who is overwhelmed and confused by her recent divorce. After graduating from high school, she worked three years as a secretary and married Ward. Since her marriage, she has not worked outside the home. She has been involved in many civic organizations such as Kiwanis and the Society for Aid to the Homeless.

June thought everything in the marriage was fine—granted, a bit dull, but fine. She and Ward had a nice house and raised two fine children. People had often commented on what a fine relationship they had. They virtually never fought with each other. As a matter of fact, things were so comfortable between them that they rarely even talked with each other anymore.

Suddenly Ward broke the news to her that he had met another woman. He told June that he loved this woman and wanted to marry her. Six months later, June found herself divorced.

Ward, forty-two, is a relatively well-to-do small businessman who owns and runs a small Pac-Man outlet store. He fell in love with Barbie, twenty-six, his attractive secretary. Ward told June that he has much more in common with Barbie than he ever had with June. He told June that he loved his children and respected her, but could no longer stay in the marriage.

June is especially concerned about her present financial status. The divorce agreement mandated that she and Ward sell their home and divide the equity. This amounted to only $8,500 for each. Her total current income is $795 per month from child support. She questions whether she can do anything other than housework. She has little confidence in her own abilities.

She always thought she would grow old with Ward, living in a nice, secure, middle-class home. Now she feels her world has been shattered.

135

Client Role:

Waleeta is a pleasant yet assertive young woman. She has many friends and has always been a loving, well-behaved child.

Waleeta is angry and disappointed with her parents. She feels they've been keeping a big secret from her. She's angry at her father for running off with another woman and angry at her mother for letting him.

She especially has difficulties when she visits her father on weekends. She resents her new stepmother, Barbie, and has frequent arguments with her.

Although Waleeta has always been a B+ student in school, her grades have been slipping recently. She can't seem to concentrate anymore. She's worried about her parents, her lack of money for clothes and activities, herself, and relationships in general. She feels that the world has let her down.

Client Role:

Beaver is really Theodore, but everybody calls him the Beaver because he's so cute. Beaver has always been a happy, active (although a bit feisty) child. He's been well-behaved, although he has had a tendency to get into minor trouble like accidentally breaking windows or losing report cards on the way home from school. Although many of his friends have tried smoking Camels and drinking Rot-a-gut apple wine, Beaver always felt this was bad and avoided "going along with the crowd."

His father's leaving really confused him. He doesn't know quite what to do. He feels frightened and insecure. He feels more tempted now to do some of the "bad" things his friends do.

C. The role-players should position themselves where the rest of the class can observe them clearly.

D. The role-play should last no longer than twenty-five minutes. Your instructor will tell you when it should stop. The workers should focus on the goals and phases cited above. The clients should do their best to play the roles assigned.

E. Observers should note their reactions during the role play on the role-play feedback form.

Role-Play Feedback Form

a. What do you think are particularly *good techniques* used by the social workers? How did the *clients react* to these techniques? (Please be specific.)

b. Do you see any weaknesses or areas in which improvement would be helpful? (Specific suggestions for how to improve are beneficial.)

c. Do you have any additional thoughts or comments?

F.   After the role-play is finished, your instructor will lead a class discussion for approximately fifteen minutes focusing on the following questions:

1.   What feedback did you note on your forms?

2.   What were the strengths of the role-play?

3.   What were some of the critical points during the role-play?

4.   What techniques did the workers use that were exceptionally helpful?

5.   What weaknesses were evident in the role-play?

6.   What suggestions do you have for improvement? Please be specific.

7.   How did the workers feel about how the role-play progressed?

8.   How did the clients feel at the critical points of the role-play?

9.   To what extent did the workers achieve their initial goals?

Focus Competencies or Practice Behaviors:
- EP 2.1.1c   Attend to professional roles and boundaries
- EP 2.1.1d   Demonstrate professional demeanor in behavior, appearance, and communication
- EP 2.1.3c   Demonstrate effective oral and written communication in working with individuals, families, groups, organizations, communities, and colleagues
- EP 2.1.10a   Substantively and affectively prepare for action with individuals, families, groups, organizations, and communities
- EP 2.1.10b   Use empathy and other interpersonal skills
- EP 2.1.10c   Develop a mutually agreed-on focus of work and desired outcomes
- EP 2.1.10d   Collect, organize, and interpret client data
- EP 2.1.10e   Assess client strengths and limitations
- EP 2.1.10f   Develop mutually agreed-on intervention goals and objectives
- EP 2.1.10g   Select appropriate intervention strategies
- EP 2.1.10j   Help clients resolve problems

Instructions:

A.   Before beginning this exercise, review the material in the text on gay/lesbian families.

B.   Read the role play described below. Volunteers are needed for each role-player. Otherwise, your instructor will assign roles.

Role-Play: A Lesbian Parent Coming Out

Social Work Role:

    The worker is a social worker at Happy Hoppy Tots, a large day care center. Her role is to address family adjustment problems involving the center's children, provide consultation regarding children's behavior to the center's "teachers," and help parents get the resources they need.

    The worker has been working with Frieda for the past six months. Frieda, thirty-one, is the mother of Angelo, four, a client at the center. The problem involved Angelo's temper tantrums. Specifically, the worker helped Frieda apply behavior modification techniques at home (for example, time-outs) and coordinated Angelo's behavior management with his teachers at the center. Improving control at home is related to improved control at the center. Angelo's behavior has significantly improved. The worker and Frieda have developed a good rapport.

Client Role:

    Frieda is a quiet, inconspicuous woman who works as a claims adjuster for an insurance company. Frieda also has another son, Harry, eight, living with her at home. She divorced Angelo and Harry's father six years ago.

    Frieda is grateful to the social worker for helping her with Angelo's temper tantrums. She is not usually one to talk about herself a lot or share her feelings. However, she has come to trust the worker and to appreciate the worker's competence.

138

> **The Situation:**
> Frieda approaches the worker one day during one of their meetings. The two have been meeting regularly to discuss Angelo's progress.
> Suddenly, Frieda blurts out to the worker, "I can't stand hiding anymore. I'm a lesbian. How can I tell my children? Can you help me?"

C.   The role-players should position themselves where the rest of the class can observe them clearly.

D.   The role-play should last no longer than twenty-five minutes. Your instructor will tell you when it should stop. The worker should focus on helping Frieda decide what to do about coming out to her children. The person playing Frieda should feel free to make up and elaborate things about her role-play life.

E.   Observers should note their reactions during the role-play on the role-play feedback form.

> **Role-Play Feedback Form**
> a.   What do you think are particularly *good techniques* used by the social workers? How did the *clients react* to these techniques? (Please be specific.)
>
> b.   Do you see any weaknesses or areas in which improvement would be helpful? (Specific suggestions for how to improve are beneficial.)
>
> c.   Do you have any additional thoughts or comments?

F.   After the role-play is finished, your instructor will lead a class discussion for approximately fifteen minutes focusing on the following questions:

1.   What feedback did you note on your forms?

2.   What were the strengths of the role-play?

3.   What were some of the critical points during the role-play?

4.   What techniques did the workers use that were exceptionally helpful?

5.   What weaknesses were evident in the role-play?

6.   What suggestions do you have for improvement? Please be specific.

7.   How did the worker feel about how the role-play progressed?

8.   How did Frieda feel at the critical points of the role-play?

9.   To what extent did the worker help Frieda make a decision about telling her children that she is a lesbian?

Focus Competencies or Practice Behaviors:

- EP 2.1.1c   Attend to professional roles and boundaries
- EP 2.1.1d   Demonstrate professional demeanor in behavior, appearance, and communication
- EP 2.1.3c   Demonstrate effective oral and written communication in working with individuals, families, groups, organizations, communities, and colleagues
- EP 2.1.10a   Substantively and affectively prepare for action with individuals, families, groups, organizations, and communities
- EP 2.1.10b   Use empathy and other interpersonal skills
- EP 2.1.10c   Develop a mutually agreed-on focus of work and desired outcomes
- EP 2.1.10d   Collect, organize, and interpret client data
- EP 2.1.10e   Assess client strengths and limitations
- EP 2.1.10f   Develop mutually agreed-on intervention goals and objectives
- EP 2.1.10g   Select appropriate intervention strategies
- EP 2.1.10j   Help clients resolve problems

Instructions:

A.   Before beginning this exercise, review chapter 10 in the text, especially the material on multiproblem families. Primary suggestions include:

    a.   Don't get overwhelmed yourself.
    b.   Follow the problem solving process as you would in any other practice situation.
    c.   Partialize and prioritize problems.
    d.   Determine which, if any, problems you can work on yourself.
    e.   Identify and use relevant community resources.

B.   Read the role-play described below. Volunteers are needed for each role-player. Otherwise, your instructor will assign roles.

Role-Play: Multiproblem Families

Social Work Role:

    The social workers are part of the family services unit in a large public welfare department in an urban county. The workers' job includes assessing the family's problems and needs, making referrals to community resources, and providing some short-term family counseling when necessary.

The Situation:

    This is the third meeting with a six-person family that has come to the department because it is plagued with a multitude of problems and doesn't know where else to turn. Individual characters and problems are described below. This information was gathered during the two prior meetings when all family members were present. The workers are now at the point of establishing a plan of action.

Client Roles:

    Ozzie, forty, spouse and father, is partially disabled in his legs because of a car accident. He can only walk for short distances and stand for short periods of time. He says he's depressed, feels useless, is unhappy, and has become quite "crabby." He describes himself normally as being rather quiet and reserved.

141

Ozzie is a high school graduate who had worked as a clerk in the city garbage collection department's office for nineteen years. He got laid off twenty-seven months ago due to departmental budget cuts. At that time, his annual salary had been $29,000.

Ozzie feels detached from his family and out of control. He has never been very involved with the children as he felt that was mostly Harriet's job.

Ozzie has defined the family's problems as follows (in unprioritized order):
- General lack of money.
- Inability to pay the rent or buy food.
- The leg is "acting up" and he needs medical attention for it, but has neither money nor insurance to pay for it.
- Almost constant fighting with Harriet.
- Feelings of inadequacy as a provider and as a husband.
- Recent sexual impotence.
- Not even enough money for booze.
- Annoyance with Grandma Hildegarde.

Harriet, thirty-two, spouse and mother, is a quiet, attractive person who has devoted her life to her family. She has an 11th grade education as she dropped out of high school to marry Ozzie. She does not consider herself to be very bright. In school, she had been placed in special education classes. She now works part-time at the Choosy Chunky Chicken Packing Plant, packing Chunky Chicken for minimum wage. Harriet has some trouble organizing household tasks and planning ahead, so she relies a lot on her mother (Grandma Hildegarde, who lives with the family) to help her make decisions.

Harriet perceives the family's problems as being the following (again in unprioritized order):
- Lack of money.
- Because of inability to pay the rent, the landlord's threatening to evict them.
- Worry over Ozzie's drinking (recently when he gets drunk, he's threatened to hit the kids).
- Fighting with Ozzie.
- Having trouble controlling the kids' behavior.
- Generally being overwhelmed and confused.

Grandma Hildegarde, sixty-nine, lives with the family for financial reasons. She expresses a generally cynical, pessimistic attitude and often dwells on "what a terrible life" she's had. She tends to interfere in Ozzie and Harriet's relationship and likes to tell them both what to do. She does love the children, especially Ricky, and likes to spend time with them. Her favorite pastime is watching daytime soap operas, especially "One Life to Live."

Hildegarde's perceptions of the family's problems include the following:
- Lack of money.
- Her social security check seems to get smaller every month.
- "Life is cruel."

142

Davida, fifteen, is Ozzie and Harriet's daughter. She is an outgoing, rebellious person to whom sarcasm comes easily. She is doing poorly in school, has flunked one grade, and has a truancy problem. She likes to stay out late with friends, especially older boys who are on probation. She was caught twice snorting coke in school. She is not one who likes to share how she really feels about things, especially her personal life and her family. She frequently fights with her parents.

The following are the problems as Davida perceives them:
- Lack of money.
- Frightened of being hit by her father when he's drunk (he's threatened her twice).
- Being sick and tired of fighting with her parents.
- Thinking that she's ugly.
- Wanting to go steady with one of the older guys she hangs out with.
- Being pretty depressed about life.
- Worry that she may be pregnant and not knowing what to do about it (she's not exactly certain who the father is).

Ricky, ten, has a shy, quiet personality. He doesn't have many friends. He maintains a C average in school. He doesn't like to do what his parents tell him to do (for example, going to bed when he's supposed to or doing the dishes). He has a close relationship with Grandma Hildegarde.

Ricky sees the problems as follows:
- Stopping his parents from constantly telling him what to do.
- Stopping his parents from fighting with each other all the time.
- Stopping his father from fighting with Grandma Hildegarde.
- Wanting more money, especially a greater weekly allowance.

Biff, thirteen, exhibits a "tough guy" attitude. He likes to be seen as the strong, mean, lean, killing machine, silent type. He doesn't say much but is usually sarcastic when he does. He's bored that he has to be involved in this interview. He doesn't feel very emotionally involved with the other members of his family except for Davida, over whom he tends to be protective. He spends most of his time with his gang, the Heavy Metals. He attends school irregularly, but has always managed to pass.

Biff's perception of the family's problems include the following:
- Wanting to "get out of here" and back to the Heavy Metals.
- Wondering how to make money almost any way he can.

C. The role-players should position themselves where the rest of the class can observe them clearly.
D. The role-play should last no longer than twenty-five minutes. Your instructor will tell you when it should stop. The workers should focus on implementing the suggestions for working with multiproblem families. The clients should portray their respective roles as best they can and elaborate details wherever they feel it's necessary.

E.   Observers should note their reactions during the role-play on the role-play feedback form below.

Role-Play Feedback Form

a.   What do you think are particularly *good techniques* used by the social workers? How did the *clients react* to these techniques? (Please be specific.)

b.   Do you see any weaknesses or areas in which improvement would be helpful? (Specific suggestions for how to improve are beneficial.)

c.   Do you have any additional thoughts or comments?

F.   After the role-play is finished, your instructor will lead a class discussion for approximately fifteen minutes, focusing on the following questions:

1.   What feedback did you note on your forms?

2.   What were the strengths of the role-play?

3.   What were some of the critical points during the role-play?

4.   What techniques did the workers use that were exceptionally helpful?

5.   What weaknesses were evident in the role-play?

144

6.   What suggestions do you have for improvement? Please be specific.

7.   How did the worker feel about how the role-play progressed?

8.   How did the clients feel at the role play's critical points?

9.   What is your impression of multiproblem families?

10.   To what extent do you feel that the family portrayed in this role-play resembles multiproblem families in real life?

11.   To what extent did the workers achieve the goals noted above for working with multiproblem families?

145

Focus Competencies or Practice Behaviors:
- EP 2.1.1c   Attend to professional roles and boundaries
- EP 2.1.1d   Demonstrate professional demeanor in behavior, appearance, and communication
- EP 2.1.3a   Distinguish, appraise, and integrate multiple sources of knowledge, including research-based knowledge and practice wisdom
- EP 2.1.3c   Demonstrate effective oral and written communication in working with individuals, families, groups, organizations, communities, and colleagues
- EP 2.1.10a   Substantively and affectively prepare for action with individuals, families, groups, organizations, and communities
- EP 2.1.10b   Use empathy and other interpersonal skills
- EP 2.1.10c   Develop a mutually agreed-on focus of work and desired outcomes
- EP 2.1.10d   Collect, organize, and interpret client data
- EP 2.1.10e   Assess client strengths and limitations
- EP 2.1.10f   Develop mutually agreed-on intervention goals and objectives
- EP 2.1.10g   Select appropriate intervention strategies
- EP 2.1.10j   Help clients resolve problems

Instructions:

A.   Select reframing or role-playing and review the related explanatory material provided in the text.

B.   Select one of the role-plays described in Exercises 1 through 3 above.

C.   Volunteers are needed to portray the worker(s) and client(s) involved in the chosen role-play. The goal will be to utilize the chosen technique within that role-play context.

D.   Continue the role-play for up to twenty minutes. By that time, the workers should have been able to implement the technique. The instructor may end the role-play earlier if the workers finish implementing the technique earlier.

E.   With the entire class, discuss for about ten minutes the following questions and issues:

1.   How was the chosen technique implemented in the role-play?

2.   What suggestions do you have to improve implementation of the technique?

3.   What did you learn about the technique from observing the role-play?

4.   How did the workers feel about implementing the technique?

5.   How did the clients feel about participating as the workers implemented the technique?

6.   How useful do you think this technique might be in real practice situations?

Chapter 10 Competencies/Practice Behaviors Exercises Assessment:

Name: _____ **Date:** _____

Supervisor's Name: _____

Focus Competencies/Practice Behaviors:

- EP 2.1.1c   Attend to professional roles and boundaries
- EP 2.1.1d   Demonstrate professional demeanor in behavior, appearance, and communication
- EP 2.1.3a   Distinguish, appraise, and integrate multiple sources of knowledge, including research-based knowledge and practice wisdom
- EP 2.1.3c   Demonstrate effective oral and written communication in working with individuals, families, groups, organizations, communities, and colleagues
- EP 2.1.10a   Substantively and affectively prepare for action with individuals, families, groups, organizations, and communities
- EP 2.1.10b   Use empathy and other interpersonal skills
- EP 2.1.10c   Develop a mutually agreed-on focus of work and desired outcomes
- EP 2.1.10d   Collect, organize, and interpret client data
- EP 2.1.10e   Assess client strengths and limitations
- EP 2.1.10f   Develop mutually agreed-on intervention goals and objectives
- EP 2.1.10g   Select appropriate intervention strategies
- EP 2.1.10j   Help clients resolve problems

Instructions:

A.   Evaluate your work or your partner's work in the Focus Competencies/Practice Behaviors by completing the Competencies/Practice Behaviors Assessment form below

B.   What other Competencies/Practice Behaviors did you use to complete these Exercises? Be sure to record them in your assessments

1.	I have attained this competency/practice behavior (in the range of 81 to 100%)
2.	I have largely attained this competency/practice behavior (in the range of 61 to 80%)
3.	I have partially attained this competency/practice behavior (in the range of 41 to 60%)
4.	I have made a little progress in attaining this competency/practice behavior (in the range of 21 to 40%)
5.	I have made almost no progress in attaining this competency/practice behavior (in the range of 0 to 20%)

EPAS 2008 Core Competencies & Core Practice Behaviors	Student Self Assessment						Evaluator Feedback
Student and Evaluator Assessment Scale and Comments	**0**	**1**	**2**	**3**	**4**	**5**	**Agree/Disagree/Comments**
EP 2.1.1 Identify as a Professional Social Worker and Conduct Oneself Accordingly:							
a. Advocate for client access to the services of social work							
b. Practice personal reflection and self-correction to assure continual professional development							
c. Attend to professional roles and boundaries							
d. Demonstrate professional demeanor in behavior, appearance, and communication							
e. Engage in career-long learning							
f. Use supervision and consultation							

148

EP 2.1.2 Apply Social Work Ethical Principles to Guide Professional Practice:						
a.	Recognize and manage personal values in a way that allows professional values to guide practice					
b.	Make ethical decisions by applying NASW Code of Ethics and, as applicable, of the IFSW/IASSW Ethics in Social Work, Statement of Principles					
c.	Tolerate ambiguity in resolving ethical conflicts					
d.	Apply strategies of ethical reasoning to arrive at principled decisions					
EP 2.1.3 Apply Critical Thinking to Inform and Communicate Professional Judgments:						
a.	Distinguish, appraise, and integrate multiple sources of knowledge, including research-based knowledge and practice wisdom					
b.	Analyze models of assessment, prevention, intervention, and evaluation					
c.	Demonstrate effective oral and written communication in working with individuals, families, groups, organizations, communities, and colleagues					
EP 2.1.4 Engage Diversity and Difference in Practice:						
a.	Recognize the extent to which a culture's structures and values may oppress, marginalize, alienate, or create or enhance privilege and power					
b.	Gain sufficient self-awareness to eliminate the influence of personal biases and values in working with diverse groups					
c.	Recognize and communicate their understanding of the importance of difference in shaping life experiences					
d.	View themselves as learners and engage those with whom they work as informants					
EP 2.1.5 Advance Human Rights and Social and Economic Justice:						
a.	Understand forms and mechanisms of oppression and discrimination					
b.	Advocate for human rights and social and economic justice					
c.	Engage in practices that advance social and economic justice					
EP 2.1.6 Engage in Research-Informed Practice and Practice-Informed Research:						
a.	Use practice experience to inform scientific inquiry					
b.	Use research evidence to inform practice					
EP 2.1.7 Apply Knowledge of Human Behavior and the Social Environment:						
a.	Utilize conceptual frameworks to guide the processes of assessment, intervention, and evaluation					
b.	Critique and apply knowledge to understand person and environment					

149

EP 2.1.8 Engage in Policy Practice to Advance Social and Economic Well-Being and to Deliver Effective Social Work Services:					
a.	Analyze, formulate, and advocate for policies that advance social well-being				
b.	Collaborate with colleagues and clients for effective policy action				
EP 2.1.9 Respond to Contexts that Shape Practice:					
a.	Continuously discover, appraise, and attend to changing locales, populations, scientific and technological developments, and emerging societal trends to provide relevant services				
b.	Provide leadership in promoting sustainable changes in service delivery and practice to improve the quality of social services				
EP 2.1.10 Engage, Assess, Intervene, and Evaluate with Individuals, Families, Groups, Organizations and Communities:					
a.	Substantively and affectively prepare for action with individuals, families, groups, organizations, and communities				
b.	Use empathy and other interpersonal skills				
c.	Develop a mutually agreed-on focus of work and desired outcomes				
d.	Collect, organize, and interpret client data				
e.	Assess client strengths and limitations				
f.	Develop mutually agreed-on intervention goals and objectives				
g.	Select appropriate intervention strategies				
h.	Initiate actions to achieve organizational goals				
i.	Implement prevention interventions that enhance client capacities				
j.	Help clients resolve problems				
k.	Negotiate, mediate, and advocate for clients				
l.	Facilitate transitions and endings				
m.	Critically analyze, monitor, and evaluate interventions				

Chapter 11
Values, Ethics, and the Resolution of Ethical Dilemmas

Competencies/Practice Behaviors Exercise 11.1
Mike Howard's Dilemma

Focus Competencies or Practice Behaviors:

- EP 2.1.2a   Recognize and manage personal values in a way that allows professional values to guide practice
- EP 2.1.2b   Make ethical decisions by applying standards of the National Association of Social Workers Code of Ethics and, as applicable, of the International Federation of Social Workers/International Association of Schools of Social Work Ethics in Social Work, Statement of Principles
- EP 2.1.2c   Tolerate ambiguity in resolving ethical conflicts
- EP 2.1.2d   Apply strategies of ethical reasoning to arrive at principled decisions

Instructions:

A.   Review the NASW Code of Ethics cited and discussed in the text which governs the professional behavior of social workers.

B.   Read the case illustration noted below and answer any questions about the activity.

Case Illustration

Mike Howard is a social worker assigned to the family services unit of the Murphy County Department of Human Services. Mike has been working at this agency for about six months. His clients are primarily young mothers who are at risk for child abuse or neglect. Deputy Sheriff Alan Simpson, a friend of Mike's from their days in high school, has contacted Mike about a recent burglary in the county. Alan believes that one of Mike's clients, Jerri Smith, has an item of stolen property in her possession. The item is a 50-inch HDTV projection television which Alan believes was stolen by Jerri's boyfriend and later given to Jerri as a gift. Alan does not believe that Jerri knows the property is stolen. He gives Mike a detailed description of the stolen set and wants Mike to check out Jerri's apartment when he visits her later this week. Mike is asked to let Deputy Simpson know if he spots the stolen set.

---

1.   Identify the ethical dilemma(s).

2.   Refer to the NASW *Code of Ethics* and appraise what professional values apply.

3.   Review the hierarchy of ethical principles, ETHICS for U, and determine which levels apply to this situation. What would you do in this situation.

4.   What is your duty to your client and to society in this case?

5.   Consider Mike's options. How might each of his choices affect his relationship with the client and his friend?

6.   To which person is his obligation greater? Why?

7.   Should Mike consult his supervisor before making a decision? Why or why not?

Focus Competencies or Practice Behaviors:

- EP 2.1.2a   Recognize and manage personal values in a way that allows professional values to guide practice
- EP 2.1.2b   Make ethical decisions by applying standards of the National Association of Social Workers Code of Ethics and, as applicable, of the International Federation of Social Workers/International Association of Schools of Social Work Ethics in Social Work, Statement of Principles
- EP 2.1.2c   Tolerate ambiguity in resolving ethical conflicts
- EP 2.1.2d   Apply strategies of ethical reasoning to arrive at principled decisions

Instructions:

A.   Review the NASW *Code of Ethics* and ETHICS for U as guides for helping you make ethical decisions.
B.   Review the case situation described below and answer the questions listed after the case situation.

Case Situation

Gemma Howser is a social worker with the Piedmont City Health Department. She is primarily responsible for doing HIV counseling with clients who have tested positive, and case management with those receiving longer-term care. Her agency is in the process of expanding services and will be hiring a new social worker. Gemma's supervisor asks her to look at the job applications as they arrive.

As Gemma reviews the job applications and résumés received for the position, she notices one from a colleague from another agency in the community. Gemma has known Zena Carson for many years and is very familiar with her education and background. What is surprising is that Zena says in her application that she has a minimum of two thousand hours in clinical work with clients, one of the job requirements for this new position. However, Gemma knows that this is not the case since none of Zena's positions since graduation has involved this type of clinical work. Moreover, a review of her résumé does not show any evidence of this experience. Gemma is troubled. She considers the following options:

1.   Call Zena and ask her about the obviously inaccurate job application.
2.   Tell her supervisor that Zena does not have the required two thousand hours and quietly have them pass over her application.
3.   File a complaint with the NASW Commission on Inquiry stating that an NASW member has misrepresented her qualifications.

---

1.   What professional values cited in the NASW *Code of Ethics* apply to this case?

2.   What ethical principles in the hierarchy ETHICS for U apply here?

3.   Are there other options which Gemma should consider?

4.   What are the advantages and disadvantages of each of these options?

5.   What are the most important issues at stake in this scenario?

6.   If you were Gemma, what would you do and why?

154

Focus Competencies or Practice Behaviors:

- EP 2.1.2a   Recognize and manage personal values in a way that allows professional values to guide practice
- EP 2.1.2b   Make ethical decisions by applying standards of the National Association of Social Workers Code of Ethics and, as applicable, of the International Federation of Social Workers/International Association of Schools of Social Work Ethics in Social Work, Statement of Principles
- EP 2.1.2c   Tolerate ambiguity in resolving ethical conflicts
- EP 2.1.2d   Apply strategies of ethical reasoning to arrive at principled decisions

Instructions:

A.   Review the case situation presented below and answer the questions listed after the case situation.

Case Situation

Judy Allison has a severe eating disorder, known as bulimia nervosa, which can be life threatening. This condition is one "in which a pathologically excessive appetite with episodic eating binges is sometimes following by purging. The purging may occur through such means as self-induced vomiting, or the abuse of laxatives, diet pills, or diuretics. Bulimia usually starts as a means of dieting."[1] She was admitted to the hospital two days ago after her sister found her unconscious in the bathroom of the home they share. As a hospital social worker, you have interviewed Judy at the request of the physician who has been treating her during her hospital stay.

Judy acknowledges she has a serious problem, but says a friend told her that it can be cured by a diet of fruits and vegetables. You are unaware of any current research for treating this illness that involves the diet she describes. Instead, you are aware of two treatment programs which have been very successful in treating this disorder. Both are multidisciplinary programs offering inpatient and outpatient treatment, individual and group therapy, and follow-up. You recommend that Judy consider entering one of these programs and offer to have a representative of the program contact her. Judy says she'd rather try the new diet her friend told her about first. She refuses further treatment.

---

1.   If you are the worker, what is your obligation, if any, to encourage and convince Judy to pursue effective treatment?

---

[1] R. Barker, *The Social Work Dictionary* (Silver Spring, MD: The National Association of Social Workers, 1995) p. 43.

2.   What professional values and ethical principles conflict in this situation?

3.   At what point (if any) does a professional have an obligation or duty to ignore the client's expressed choice?

4.   If you determined (after proper consultation) that Judy's new diet could be life-threatening, what would you do?

Competencies/Practice Behaviors Exercise 11.4
What Is the Ethical Thing to Do?

Focus Competencies or Practice Behaviors:
- EP 2.1.2a   Recognize and manage personal values in a way that allows professional values to guide practice
- EP 2.1.2b   Make ethical decisions by applying standards of the National Association of Social Workers Code of Ethics and, as applicable, of the International Federation of Social Workers/International Association of Schools of Social Work Ethics in Social Work, Statement of Principles
- EP 2.1.2c   Tolerate ambiguity in resolving ethical conflicts
- EP 2.1.2d   Apply strategies of ethical reasoning to arrive at principled decisions

Instructions:
A.   Review the material on ethical standards proposed by the NASW *Code of Ethics* and on the hierarchy of ethical principles ETHICS for U.
B.   Read the following ethical dilemmas and propose alternative solutions for half of them. From those possible solutions, choose the one you believe is the best for each dilemma. Explain your reasons for your choice.

156

Ethical Dilemma #1

Yvonne is a child protective services worker. After receiving a referral, she or other assigned workers will "investigate reports of child abuse and neglect, assess the degree of harm and the ongoing risk of harm to the child, determine whether the child can remain safely in the home or should be placed in the custody of the state, and work closely with the family or juvenile court regarding appropriate plans for the child's safety and well-being"(Liederman, 1995, p. 425).

Yvonne has a client, Lolita, four, who was allegedly abused by both parents. Lolita currently resides with her mother, Reza, while Reza is receiving counseling and other services including job training. Bill, Lolita's father, no longer lives in the home but has told Yvonne he would like to seek custody of Lolita. Bill calls Yvonne to complain about Reza's treatment of Lolita. He states that Lolita often wets her bed at night and Reza simply ignores it. Reza subsequently allows Lolita to sleep in her wet bed. Then, even worse, the next day or night Reza does not change the sheets for Lolita. Yvonne notes carefully what Bill tells her in Lolita's case record.

The next day, Reza calls Yvonne in a panic. She cries that Bill is threatening to take Lolita away from her. Reza says Bill told her he called Yvonne to complain about Reza's treatment of Lolita. Reza stresses that she does not want to lose her little girl. She demands to see Yvonne's records.

1.   What should Yvonne do: Show Reza the incriminating records, or not?

Ethical Dilemma #2

Herman is a substance abuse counselor. He is currently seeing an alcoholic client, Anne, age thirty-seven. Herman views Anne as a timid, needy woman who is working on increasing her self-esteem, problem solving skills, and assertiveness in the context of addressing her alcoholism problem. Treatment is going exceptionally well. Anne has not been drinking for months and has been attending Alcoholics Anonymous meetings regularly. Anne is very grateful to Herman for all she feels he has done for her. One day at the end of the counseling session, Anne walks up to Herman and says, "I really need a hug!" What should Herman do? On the one hand, Anne is needy of approval and affection. She wishes to convey her gratitude to Herman. On the other, he does not want to convey inappropriate feelings that do not exist.

2.   Should he allow her to hug him or not?

Ethical Dilemma #3

Sue married Jim two years after the biological father of her daughter Andrea disappeared seemingly from the face of the earth. They have now been married for seven years. Andrea, eight, and Jim have become very close. Jim feels just like Andrea is his biological daughter. Jim and Sue pursue the possibility of Jim adopting Andrea. Mary Ellen is the adoptions worker assigned to the case. She helps with the relatively complex process of having the biological father relinquish his parental rights for Andrea when he is nowhere to be found. Mary Ellen has completed a number of stepparent adoptions and has become quite competent in their successful completion. Jim and Sue are very thankful. They give Mary Ellen a $50 gift certificate for a popular local restaurant.

3. Is this appropriate or not? Should Mary Ellen keep the gift or return it? What is the ethical and tactful thing to do?

Ethical Dilemma #4

Lloyd is a social worker at a group home for people who are cognitively challenged or have cognitive disabilities (the former, more negative term is mentally retarded).[3] Ellie, thirty-five, has been a resident at the group home for eight years. She has relatively high adaptive functioning in terms of daily living skills, can read at the fourth grade level, and has successfully worked at a sheltered workshop since entering the group home. She has no known relatives. The court has designated a lawyer as her guardian *ad litem* (that is, a court appointee whose responsibility is to "preserve and manage the affairs of another person who is considered incapable of managing his or her own affairs," especially when court actions are involved) (Barker, 1995, p. 158).

Without warning, Ellie cheerfully approaches Lloyd one day and informs him that she has saved enough money to go to Disney World, her dream of a lifetime. She chatters on about getting the tickets and taking her first airplane ride. Lloyd is familiar with Ellie's capabilities and strongly feels this endeavor is far beyond her capabilities.

---

[3] *Cognitively challenged* is an alternative term referring to mental retardation. *Mental retardation* is "significantly below-average intellectual functioning and potential, with onset before age 18, resulting in limitation in communication, self-care and self-direction, home living, social and interpersonal skills, use of community resources, academic skills, work, leisure, health, and safety" (Barker, 1995, p. 232). Many professionals feel that referring to such individuals as being cognitively challenged is far more positive than using the term mentally retarded (DeWeaver, 1995).

158

4.   What should he do?

Ethical Dilemma #5

Ricardo is a social services worker who specializes in teaching parents effective child management skills. Over the past six months, he has been working with Irma, a former crack user, to gain control of her four children's behavior. Although it was very difficult at first for Irma to trust Ricardo, they now have established a trusting relationship in which Irma feels free to discuss difficult issues with Ricardo. Ideally, Ricardo would like to continue work with Irma for the next several months. However, he has been transferred to another unit's position with a higher salary. Irma has achieved many of the major goals, but still could make significant improvements in how she treats her children. Ricardo feels it would be very difficult for Irma to become accustomed to and work with another worker.

---

5.   What should he do?

Ethical Dilemma #6

Nick is a counselor for teenagers with severe emotional and behavioral problems who reside in a residential treatment center. He sees himself as a shy person who finds it difficult to confront issues in conflictual situations. As a member of an interdisciplinary team, he attends a staffing for one of his clients at which progress is reviewed and future plans established. Dr. Schmaltz, the psychiatrist attending the meeting, is a powerful, authoritarian man who makes strong points completely in opposition to what Nick is proposing for the client being reviewed. Dr. Schmaltz commands much authority and respect among other staff.

---

6.   What should Nick do?

Ethical Dilemma #7

Chuck is a youth counselor at an urban YMCA.[4] He is in his early twenties, good at sports, familiar with young people's jargon, and, thus, extremely popular with his teenage clientele. Emilio is another youth counselor at the same agency. One night after work, Emilio accidentally observes Chuck smoking a joint with two of his clients in the shadows of an alley. After serious thought, the next day Emilio confronts Chuck about his behavior. Chuck responds that it was only marijuana and it provided a way for him to "join with" and be accepted by some of his clients. Chuck rationalizes that smoking joints prevents many young people from using harder, more dangerous drugs. Chuck implies that Emilio is just jealous of Chuck's good rapport with the clientele.

7.   What should Emilio do now?

Ethical Dilemma #8

Willie Lee, twenty-three, is a resident in a center for people who have cognitive disabilities. Willie Lee can eat by himself and take care of most of his daily hygiene needs. His vocabulary is small, but he usually understands much more than he can express. Willie Lee is a very friendly person who socializes well with peers and is generally respectful of staff. He looks forward to his father's rare visits, sometimes only once or twice a year. His mother died at his birth.

Willie Lee's father, Horace, has recently remarried and is moving across the continent. He has hired an attorney and wants to terminate his guardianship and responsibility for Willie Lee. Horace has always found Willie Lee a burden and been embarrassed by his disability. Horace feels this is his chance to abandon the whole problem and not think about it anymore. Although Willie Lee is always happy when Horace visits, he never asks about him. This may be partially due to Willie Lee's communication difficulties.

Horace succeeds in terminating his rights and moves away. He informs the center that he plans on having no further contact with Willie Lee.

---

[4] *YMCA* refers to the Young Men's Christian Association. They are a "worldwide group of organizations devoted to the physical, intellectual, social, and spiritual well-being of young men" (Barker, 1995, p. 413). One should note that they no longer restrict themselves to Christians.

8. Should the center social worker inform Willie Lee of this turn of events? Does Willie Lee have the right to know about his father's status?

Ethical Dilemma #9

Ling, eighty-six, is a bed-bound resident in a nursing home. Although she has numerous physical difficulties, she has maintained fairly strong mental faculties. She enjoys the company of her two daughters who visit regularly. Ling's physician has just discovered that Ling has developed a lethal form of intestinal cancer and has only weeks, possibly a few months, to live. Ling's daughters beg the nursing home social worker not to tell Ling of her condition. They plan to visit Ling daily and want her to enjoy her time as best she can. They feel that informing her about the cancer would only ruin her last days.

---

9. What should the social worker do? Should she inform Ling of her condition? What are the pros and cons of informing or not informing?

Ethical Dilemma #10

Sissy is a financial assistance worker. Agency policy requires her to report any extra income clients may earn. The exact amount of such income is then deducted from their financial assistance checks. An excited client, Bertha, with four children, burst out, "I'm so happy! My neighbor is going to pay me to take care of her two children while she works. This will do wonders for my grocery bill."

---

10. As her worker, what should Sissy do? Should she report the additional income and thereby decrease her financial assistance check? If so, should she tell Bertha what she plans to do? What might Bertha's reaction be? Or should Sissy keep her statement confidential, thereby disobeying agency policy? What is the ethical thing to do?

Ethical Dilemma #11

Chuck works for a social services agency serving almost all Hispanic and African American clients. All the social workers and administrators are white. None of the professional staff speak Spanish.[5] Chuck is very concerned about this situation, but hesitates to make waves. It is such a major problem. He feels too insignificant to take it on himself. Yet, he can't keep it from bothering him.

How might clients be better served? What are the agency's needs? What options might Chuck consider pursuing? What is the ethical thing to do?

---

11. How might clients be better served? What are the agency's needs? What options might Chuck consider pursuing? What is the ethical thing to do?

Ethical Dilemma #12

Lai is a social worker at a shelter and treatment center for runaways. The center typically uses volunteers to serve many of its functions, including counseling youth and families. Although volunteers receive twenty hours of training, Lai feel this does not make them competent to counsel young people and their families.

---

[5] This vignette is adapted from one presented in B. Cournoyer, *The Social Work Skills Workbook*, 2nd ed. (Pacific Grove, CA: Brooks/Cole, 1996) p. 72.

12. What, if anything, is wrong with this agency's volunteer policy? What might Lai do to make changes? What might those changes be? What is the ethical thing to do?

<hr>

Competencies/Practice Behaviors Exercise 11.5
A Dual Relationship Questionnaire—Clients and Supervisors

Focus Competencies or Practice Behaviors:
- EP 2.1.1c Attend to professional roles and boundaries
- EP 2.1.1f Use supervision and consultation
- EP 2.1.2a Recognize and manage personal values in a way that allows professional values to guide practice
- EP 2.1.2c Tolerate ambiguity in resolving ethical conflicts
- EP 2.1.2d Apply strategies of ethical reasoning to arrive at principled decisions

Instructions:
A. Fill out the following questionnaire. Note that it involves opinions about dual relationships with current clients, former clients, current supervisors, and former supervisors. Circle from 1 to 4 what you consider the best answer for each question. This will take about 10 minutes.
B. When you've finished, add up your scores for each section and divide that total by 6. The result is an average score indicating how much you feel dual relationships with clients or supervisors are appropriate or inappropriate, 1 being never appropriate and 4 being always appropriate.
C. When you are finished, answer the questions below the questionnaire.

<hr>

DUAL RELATIONSHIP QUESTIONNAIRE
CURRENT CLIENTS:
1. Is it appropriate and ethical for a professional social worker to become friends with a client while working with that client?

1	2	3	4
Never	Infrequently	Sometimes	Always

2. Is it appropriate and ethical for a social worker to accept an invitation to a special event (e.g., wedding or graduation) from a current client?

1	2	3	4
Never	Infrequently	Sometimes	Always

3. Is it appropriate and ethical to accept a gift from a client (e.g., as a thank you or for Christmas or birthday)?

1	2	3	4
Never	Infrequently	Sometimes	Always

163

4. Is it appropriate and ethical for a social worker to go out to lunch or dinner with a current client after a counseling session?

1	2	3	4
Never	Infrequently	Sometimes	Always

5. Is it appropriate and ethical for a social worker to invite a current client to a personal party or social event?

1	2	3	4
Never	Infrequently	Sometimes	Always

6. Is it appropriate and ethical for a social worker to invite current clients to an agency function such as an open house?

1	2	3	4
Never	Infrequently	Sometimes	Always

Total _____/6=_____

FORMER CLIENTS:

7. Is it appropriate and ethical for a social worker to become friends with a client after their professional relationship has ended?

1	2	3	4
Never	Infrequently	Sometimes	Always

8. Is it appropriate and ethical for a social worker to accept an invitation to a special event (e.g., wedding or graduation) from a former client?

1	2	3	4
Never	Infrequently	Sometimes	Always

9. Is it appropriate and ethical to accept a gift from a former client (e.g., as a thank you or for Christmas or birthday)?

1	2	3	4
Never	Infrequently	Sometimes	Always

10. Is it appropriate and ethical for a social worker to invite a former client to a personal party or social event?

1	2	3	4
Never	Infrequently	Sometimes	Always

11. Is it appropriate and ethical for a social worker to go out to lunch or dinner with a former client?

1	2	3	4
Never	Infrequently	Sometimes	Always

12. Is it appropriate and ethical for a social worker to become involved in a sexual relationship with a former client?

1	2	3	4
Never	Infrequently	Sometimes	Always

Total _____/6=_____

CURRENT SUPERVISORS

13. Is it appropriate and ethical for a worker to become friends with her current supervisor ?

1	2	3	4
Never	Infrequently	Sometimes	Always

14. Is it appropriate and ethical for a social worker to accept an invitation to a special event (e.g., wedding or graduation) from a current supervisor?

1	2	3	4
Never	Infrequently	Sometimes	Always

15. Is it appropriate and ethical to accept a gift from or give one to a current supervisor (e.g., as a thank you or for Christmas or birthday)?

1	2	3	4
Never	Infrequently	Sometimes	Always

16. Is it appropriate and ethical for a social worker to go out to lunch or dinner with a current supervisor?

1	2	3	4
Never	Infrequently	Sometimes	Always

17. Is it appropriate and ethical for a social worker to invite a current supervisor to a personal party or social event?

1	2	3	4
Never	Infrequently	Sometimes	Always

18. Is it appropriate and ethical for a social worker to become involved in a sexual relationship with a current supervisor?

1	2	3	4
Never	Infrequently	Sometimes	Always

Total _____/6=_____

FORMER SUPERVISORS

19. Is it appropriate and ethical for a worker to become friends with a former supervisor?

1	2	3	4
Never	Infrequently	Sometimes	Always

20. Is it appropriate and ethical for a social worker to accept an invitation to a special event (e.g., wedding or graduation) from a former supervisor?

1	2	3	4
Never	Infrequently	Sometimes	Always

21. Is it appropriate and ethical to accept a gift from or give one to a former supervisor (e.g., as a thank you or for Christmas or birthday)?

1	2	3	4
Never	Infrequently	Sometimes	Always

165

22. Is it appropriate and ethical for a social worker to go out to lunch or dinner with a former supervisor?

1	2	3	4
Never	Infrequently	Sometimes	Always

23. Is it appropriate and ethical for a social worker to invite a former supervisor to a personal party or social event?

1	2	3	4
Never	Infrequently	Sometimes	Always

24. Is it appropriate and ethical for a social worker to become involved in a sexual relationship with a former supervisor after their professional relationship has ended?

1	2	3	4
Never	Infrequently	Sometimes	Always

Total _____ /6=_____

1.　What were your average scores for each section?

2.　What were the differences among current and former clients, and current and former supervisors?

3.　What were the reasons for these differences?

4.　What questions, if any, did you find particularly difficult to answer? Explain why.

5.　What did you learn from this questionnaire about issues you might encounter in practice?

166

Focus Competencies or Practice Behaviors:
- EP 2.1.1c   Attend to professional roles and boundaries
- EP 2.1.1f   Use supervision and consultation
- EP 2.1.2a   Recognize and manage personal values in a way that allows professional values to guide practice
- EP 2.1.2c   Tolerate ambiguity in resolving ethical conflicts
- EP 2.1.2d   Apply strategies of ethical reasoning to arrive at principled decisions

Instructions:

A.   Read the following vignettes and discuss the questions that are listed for each vignette.

> **Vignette #1**
> "A male social work student presented a dozen red roses to his female field instructor on the last day of supervision and one month later they were engaged. At the risk of being unromantic, one can question the quality of her social work supervision throughout the year if there had been a growing personal relationship" (Congress, 1996, p. 334).

1.   To what extent is the behavior portrayed in each scenario ethical?

2.   What are the potential positive and negative consequences of the behaviors involved?

3.   What should the professional social worker(s) involved have or have not done?

1. To what extent is the behavior portrayed in each scenario ethical?

2. What are the potential positive and negative consequences of the behaviors involved?

3. What should the professional social worker(s) involved have or have not done?

1.   To what extent is the behavior portrayed in each scenario ethical?

2.   What are the potential positive and negative consequences of the behaviors involved?

3.   What should the professional social worker(s) involved have or have not done?

Vignette #4

   A Social Work Club holds annual banquets for its members and invites faculty, who usually attend. Often, faculty and students meet in the bar for cocktails and cokes before the banquet begins. Conversations are informal and mildly personal in terms of focusing on non-academic topics.

---

1.   To what extent is the behavior portrayed in each scenario ethical?

2.   What are the potential positive and negative consequences of the behaviors involved?

3.   What should the professional social worker(s) involved have or have not done?

Vignette #5

Petula, a female professor, was Burt's advisor throughout his four years of college in addition to being his instructor for several courses. Upon meeting they immediately developed a good rapport. They came from the same town and both had a straightforward, "say it like it is" personal communication style. Throughout his college career, they addressed various academic issues in addition to discussing some personal problems. He had cerebral palsy which sometimes limited his ready access to campus resources and made dating more difficult because of discrimination.

Burt graduated with his BSW and immediately went on for his MSW. Upon completion Burt called Petula and volunteered to serve as a speaker in one of her courses. She invited him, and he did a nice job. Afterwards, she invited him to lunch which she did with all her speakers. Over the next ten years, Petula invited him to speak each semester. Over time they became good friends, comfortable in discussing many topics ranging from family problems to vacation plans to financial worries to professional issues. Petula occasionally invited Burt to social events at her home.

---

1.   To what extent is the behavior portrayed in each scenario ethical?

2.   What are the potential positive and negative consequences of the behaviors involved?

3.   What should the professional social worker(s) involved have or have not done?

Vignette #6

Alicia, 32, originally from Ecuador, was bilingual. She consistently expressed feelings of inferiority and felt her peers were exceptionally critical of her due to her accent. Chantrell, one of her instructors, met several times with Alicia over the course of the two semesters at Alicia's request. They focused on Alicia's many strengths and helping her develop ways to deal with her classmates. Alicia made two trips back to her home in Ecuador during this period. Each time she brought Chantrell some small gifts of coffee or local handicrafts which Chantrell accepted.

1. To what extent is the behavior portrayed in each scenario ethical?

2. What are the potential positive and negative consequences of the behaviors involved?

3. What should the professional social worker(s) involved have or have not done?

> Earl, a county social services supervisor, who took his supervisee Carla, a relatively new MSW with one year's experience, under his wing. Earl genuinely liked Carla, her enthusiasm, and her serious desire to do the best job possible. He took her on home visits to provide a role model for how these should be done. At her request, he helped her develop counseling techniques and write efficient, effective reports. In some ways, he assumed the role of friend with her. For example, when he held a party for all his supervisees and co-workers, he asked her to help him with the arrangements, which she gladly did. Carla respected and admired Earl. At one point, she felt she was even falling in love with him, although Earl never felt any reciprocal romantic feelings toward her (they were both single). Eventually, Earl left the agency for another position. Twenty-five years later Carla still thinks fondly of Earl and appreciates all he taught her. Carla, by the way, is happily married to somebody else.

1. To what extent is the behavior portrayed in each scenario ethical?

2. What are the potential positive and negative consequences of the behaviors involved?

3. What should the professional social worker(s) involved have or have not done?

Focus Competencies or Practice Behaviors:
- EP 2.1.1c   Attend to professional roles and boundaries
- EP 2.1.2a   Recognize and manage personal values in a way that allows professional values to guide practice
- EP 2.1.2c   Tolerate ambiguity in resolving ethical conflicts
- EP 2.1.2d   Apply strategies of ethical reasoning to arrive at principled decisions

Instructions:

A.   Read the following ethical dilemmas and discuss the questions that are listed after each scenario.

> **Ethical Dilemma #1:** Fernando is a substance abuse counselor who had been working with his client Trixie for several years. Trixie attributes much of her success in maintaining sobriety to Fernando's help and efforts. Fernando receives an invitation to Trixie's wedding with a note saying how much it would mean to Trixie for him to attend.

1.   What is the worker's professional role and what are the boundary issues involved?

2.   What emotions, wants, and needs might characterize the worker involved in the scenario?

3.   What alternatives are available for the worker to take?

4.   What are the potential positive and negative consequences for each alternative?

5.   How might each alternative affect the client and the worker/client relationship?

6.   What course of action should the worker take that is the most ethical and appropriate for both worker and client? Explain why.

Ethical Dilemma #2: Kasinda, a hospice social worker, visits her 72-year-old hospice client Leona weekly to provide supportive counseling and link her with needed resources. One week Leona invites Kasinda to have lunch with her.

1.   What is the worker's professional role and what are the boundary issues involved?

2.   What emotions, wants, and needs might characterize the worker involved in the scenario?

3.   What alternatives are available for the worker to take?

174

4.   What are the potential positive and negative consequences for each alternative?

5.   How might each alternative affect the client and the worker/client relationship?

6.   What course of action should the worker take that is the most ethical and appropriate for both worker and client? Explain why.

Ethical Dilemma #3: Darwin, a private practitioner in a rural area, provides counseling on a range of issues. Gilbert, his client for two years, addressed serious self-esteem issues during the course of counseling. Partially as a result of the counseling Gilbert went back to school and earned a BSW and MSW. Six years after his counseling ended, Gilbert approaches Darwin and asks him to provide clinical supervision. Gilbert expresses how much he respects Darwin and how no other MSWs are available in the area.

---

1.   What is the worker's professional role and what are the boundary issues involved?

2.   What emotions, wants, and needs might characterize the worker involved in the scenario?

3.   What alternatives are available for the worker to take?

4.   What are the potential positive and negative consequences for each alternative?

5.   How might each alternative affect the client and the worker/client relationship?

6.   What course of action should the worker take that is the most ethical and appropriate for both worker and client? Explain why.

Ethical Dilemma #4: Freddy, 55, has a cognitive disability, an IQ within the borderline range, and a serious speech impediment. He can live by himself in a small Midwestern town with regular support from the local Center for People with Cognitive Disabilities. His sister Farrah and her family are also very involved with his life, although they live four hours away.

Freddy has lived in this small town all his life and does not want to leave and live elsewhere even to join his family. Shirley, his assigned social worker at the center, has been very helpful by making regular home visits to make sure things were going smoothly, setting up appropriate vocational testing, helping Freddy get involved in regular social and recreational activities at the center, and getting him a part-time job at Don's Dinky Diner, a local restaurant.

Freddy's family is very thankful to Shirley for her help. It would be very difficult for Farrah and other family members to visit Freddy on a weekly basis as Shirley does. Farrah gives Shirley a $30.00 gift certificate to the local All-Mart store as an appreciation gift before the Christmas holidays.

1. What is the worker's professional role and what are the boundary issues involved?

2. What emotions, wants, and needs might characterize the worker involved in the scenario?

3. What alternatives are available for the worker to take?

4. What are the potential positive and negative consequences for each alternative?

5.   How might each alternative affect the client and the worker/client relationship?

6.   What course of action should the worker take that is the most ethical and appropriate for both worker and client? Explain why.

Ethical Dilemma #5: Jennifer, 23, is a student working at a halfway house for men on parole who are also substance abusers. This is part of her final 480 hour field internship. Jennifer is very attracted to Sly, a 26-year-old, handsome client who is also quite charming. She finds it very difficult to avoid responding to his flattering, flirtatious advances. She is halfway through her placement and is finding it extremely difficult not to respond to Sly and secretly date him. The agency has a strict policy that no worker should date a client within six months after either have left the agency. Jennifer finds herself preoccupied thinking about him much of the time. She feels that she's losing control.

---

1.   What is the worker's professional role and what are the boundary issues involved?

2.   What emotions, wants, and needs might characterize the worker involved in the scenario?

3.　　What alternatives are available for the worker to take?

4.　　What are the potential positive and negative consequences for each alternative?

5.　　How might each alternative affect the client and the worker/client relationship?

6.　　What course of action should the worker take that is the most ethical and appropriate for both worker and client? Explain why.

Competencies/Practice Behaviors Exercise 11.8
HELP! The NASW Code of Ethics

Focus Competencies or Practice Behaviors:
- EP 2.1.2a　　Recognize and manage personal values in a way that allows professional values to guide practice
- EP 2.1.2b　　Make ethical decisions by applying standards of the National Association of Social Workers Code of Ethics and, as applicable, of the International Federation of Social Workers/International Association of Schools of Social Work Ethics in Social Work, Statement of Principles
- EP 2.1.2c　　Tolerate ambiguity in resolving ethical conflicts
- EP 2.1.2d　　Apply strategies of ethical reasoning to arrive at principled decisions

Instructions:

A.   Read the following citations from the NASW Code of Ethics.

B.   Evaluate how each section relates to the scenarios described earlier in Exercise 7 by responding to the questions provided below.

WORKERS AND CLIENTS

The NASW Code of Ethics (NASW, 2008) states:

"Social workers should not engage in dual or multiple relationships with clients or former clients in which there is a risk of exploitation or potential harm to the client. In instances when dual or multiple relationships are unavoidable, social workers should take steps to protect clients and are responsible for setting clear, appropriate, and culturally sensitive boundaries. (Dual or multiple relationships occur when social workers relate to clients in more than one relationship, whether professional, social, or business. Dual or multiple relationships can occur simultaneously or consecutively.)"(1.06c).

"Social workers should under no circumstances engage in sexual activities or sexual contact with current clients, whether such contact is consensual or forced" (1.09a).

Review Ethical Dilemma #5 in Exercise 7 above and answer the following questions:

1.   To what extent does the Code provide clear direction regarding what workers should do in each vignette?

2.   For what aspects of each dilemma must workers use their own discretion regarding what behavior is ethical and what is not?

3.   According to the Code, what do you think the worker should do?

INSTRUCTORS AND STUDENTS

The NASW Code of Ethics states:

"Social workers who function as educators or field instructors for students should not engage in any dual or multiple relationships with students in which there is a risk of exploitation or potential harm to the student. Social work educators and field instructors are responsible for setting clear, appropriate, and culturally sensitive boundaries" (3.02d).

Review the Ethical Dilemma #3 cited in Exercise 7 above and answer the following questions:

1.   To what extent does the Code provide clear direction regarding what supervisors and workers should do in each vignette?

2.   For what aspects of each dilemma must supervisors and workers use their own discretion regarding what behavior is ethical and what is not?

181

3.   According to the Code, what do you think the supervisor and worker should do?

Competencies/Practice Behaviors Exercise 11.9
Role Play: What Would You Say and Why?

Focus Competencies or Practice Behaviors:
- EP 2.1.1c   Attend to professional roles and boundaries
- EP 2.1.2a   Recognize and manage personal values in a way that allows professional values to guide practice
- EP 2.1.2b   Make ethical decisions by applying standards of the National Association of Social Workers Code of Ethics and, as applicable, of the International Federation of Social Workers/International Association of Schools of Social Work Ethics in Social Work, Statement of Principles
- EP 2.1.2c   Tolerate ambiguity in resolving ethical conflicts
- EP 2.1.2d   Apply strategies of ethical reasoning to arrive at principled decisions
- EP 2.1.3c   Demonstrate effective oral and written communication in working with individuals, families, groups, organizations, communities, and colleagues
- EP 2.1.10a   Substantively and affectively prepare for action with individuals, families, groups, organizations, and communities
- EP 2.1.10b   Use empathy and other interpersonal skills
- EP 2.1.10c   Develop a mutually agreed-on focus of work and desired outcomes
- EP 2.1.10d   Collect, organize, and interpret client data
- EP 2.1.10e   Assess client strengths and limitations
- EP 2.1.10f   Develop mutually agreed-on intervention goals and objectives
- EP 2.1.10g   Select appropriate intervention strategies
- EP 2.1.10j   Help clients resolve problems

Instructions:
A.   Review the material on dual relationships.
B.   Role play each of the following scenarios with another classmate, switching roles after each one.
C.   Think about what you would do if you were the worker.
D.   For each, you should begin the role play with the client making the comments or asking the worker designated questions as indicated in the scenario. Allow about five minutes to conduct the role play, and then answer the questions following the last scenario.

182

SCENARIO #1

Harriett, the Worker: You're a worker at a nursing home who has spent significant amounts of time with Polly, a delightful 83-year-old. She sincerely appreciates your time and maintains a good sense of humor despite her increasingly failing health. You've helped link her to a variety of resources, arranged for her to participate in a number of the home's activities including outings, and have helped her work out some personal issues with her daughter Pru. You genuinely like and respect Polly who maintains such a positive attitude despite her health problems.

Polly, the Client: You've always seen yourself as a positive person who enjoys and appreciates the other people around you. At 83 you continue striving to appreciate the positive elements in life. You are finding it increasingly difficult to get around easily, even using your walker, and are suffering from increasing pain caused by a number of gastrointestinal and other difficulties. You really like Harriett who always seems to have time for you and has helped you work out some difficult issues. You'd love to have her join you at your 84th birthday party over at Pru's next Saturday. You don't know how many more special occasions, if any, you have left. You're going to invite Harriett, that's all that's to it.

SCENARIO #2

Ashanti, the Worker: You are a social worker at a shelter for battered women. You've been working closely with Fola, one of your clients, for over six months now. With her two small children, she has left her abusive spouse, found an apartment, and started a new job training program. You've helped her get the appropriate financial assistance to get her started on the road to independence. You genuinely like her and respect her for her courage in getting through the rough times she's had. Occasionally, you think you might have become friends in some other non-professional context.

Fola, the Client: You have finally gotten your act together and are on your way to a strong and independent future with your children. The only bad thing is that you will sincerely miss Ashanti, who has helped you work out many aspects of your life. In another two weeks, she will no longer be formally involved as your worker. You feel you have developed a meaningful friendship with her and would like to keep in touch. You're going to ask her to continue to be her friend. At least you could keep in touch by phone and occasionally go out to lunch or to a movie together.

SCENARIO #3[1]

Carlton, the Worker: Carlton is a substance abuse counselor working for a private social services agency. Bob, a car mechanic, has been one of his clients for almost a year. Carlton has assisted Bob in making many life changes and establishing a life of sobriety. Carlton feels they have a good and productive relationship. This is despite the fact that sometimes Bob has missed his payments due to the financial problems resulting from prior years of substance abuse. Bob always eventually pays his bills when he can.

---

[1] This scenario is loosely based on one discussed in *Social Work Values and Ethics* by E. P. Congress (Chicago: Nelson-Hall, 1996, p. 111).

One day Carlton has unexpected car trouble and so is forced to cancel an appointment with Bob. Carlton calls the agency and an administrative assistant calls Bob about the cancellation, briefly explaining the reason. During their informal initial greeting right before their next counseling session, Bob asks Carlton what was wrong with his car and Carlton briefly explains.

Bob, the Client: Bob thinks very highly of Carlton who has helped him get through some very rough times. Bob considers himself an excellent mechanic who works for a local gas station and garage that does a good business in auto repair. When he hears about Carlton's car problems, he eagerly volunteers to give the car a good check-up and make certain the repairs would be done right. All Carlton needs to do is to bring the car in. He feels this would be a way to repay Carlton a little in a personal way for all the help Carlton's given. Bob thinks silently to himself that he might even be able to do this for free on his own time or, at least, give Carlton a greatly cut rate. Bob makes the suggestion to Carlton.

1. What were the boundary issues involved?

2. How did you, as the worker, feel during the role play?

3. What did you, as the worker, decide to do?

4.   What was the ethical thing to do and why?

5.   How did you, as the client, feel at the end of the role play?

6.   What have you learned from this role play about dual relationships?

Chapter 11 Competencies/Practice Behaviors Exercises Assessment:

Name: _____ Date: _____

Supervisor's Name: _____

Focus Competencies/Practice Behaviors:

- EP 2.1.1c   Attend to professional roles and boundaries
- EP 2.1.1f   Use supervision and consultation
- EP 2.1.2a   Recognize and manage personal values in a way that allows professional values to guide practice
- EP 2.1.2b   Make ethical decisions by applying standards of the National Association of Social Workers Code of Ethics and, as applicable, of the International Federation of Social Workers/International Association of Schools of Social Work Ethics in Social Work, Statement of Principles
- EP 2.1.2c   Tolerate ambiguity in resolving ethical conflicts
- EP 2.1.2d   Apply strategies of ethical reasoning to arrive at principled decisions
- EP 2.1.3c   Demonstrate effective oral and written communication in working with individuals, families, groups, organizations, communities, and colleagues
- EP 2.1.10a   Substantively and affectively prepare for action with individuals, families, groups, organizations, and communities
- EP 2.1.10b   Use empathy and other interpersonal skills
- EP 2.1.10c   Develop a mutually agreed-on focus of work and desired outcomes
- EP 2.1.10d   Collect, organize, and interpret client data
- EP 2.1.10e   Assess client strengths and limitations
- EP 2.1.10f   Develop mutually agreed-on intervention goals and objectives
- EP 2.1.10g   Select appropriate intervention strategies
- EP 2.1.10j   Help clients resolve problems

Instructions:

A.   Evaluate your work or your partner's work in the Focus Competencies/Practice Behaviors by completing the Competencies/Practice Behaviors Assessment form below

B.   What other Competencies/Practice Behaviors did you use to complete these Exercises? Be sure to record them in your assessments

1.	I have attained this competency/practice behavior (in the range of 81 to 100%)
2.	I have largely attained this competency/practice behavior (in the range of 61 to 80%)
3.	I have partially attained this competency/practice behavior (in the range of 41 to 60%)
4.	I have made a little progress in attaining this competency/practice behavior (in the range of 21 to 40%)
5.	I have made almost no progress in attaining this competency/practice behavior (in the range of 0 to 20%)

EPAS 2008 Core Competencies & Core Practice Behaviors							Student Self Assessment						Evaluator Feedback
Student and Evaluator Assessment Scale and Comments							0	1	2	3	4	5	Agree/Disagree/Comments
EP 2.1.1 Identify as a Professional Social Worker and Conduct Oneself Accordingly:													
a. Advocate for client access to the services of social work													
b. Practice personal reflection and self-correction to assure continual professional development													

186

c.	Attend to professional roles and boundaries						
d.	Demonstrate professional demeanor in behavior, appearance, and communication						
e.	Engage in career-long learning						
f.	Use supervision and consultation						
EP 2.1.2 Apply Social Work Ethical Principles to Guide Professional Practice:							
a.	Recognize and manage personal values in a way that allows professional values to guide practice						
b.	Make ethical decisions by applying NASW Code of Ethics and, as applicable, of the IFSW/IASSW Ethics in Social Work, Statement of Principles						
c.	Tolerate ambiguity in resolving ethical conflicts						
d.	Apply strategies of ethical reasoning to arrive at principled decisions						
EP 2.1.3 Apply Critical Thinking to Inform and Communicate Professional Judgments:							
a.	Distinguish, appraise, and integrate multiple sources of knowledge, including research-based knowledge and practice wisdom						
b.	Analyze models of assessment, prevention, intervention, and evaluation						
c.	Demonstrate effective oral and written communication in working with individuals, families, groups, organizations, communities, and colleagues						
EP 2.1.4 Engage Diversity and Difference in Practice:							
a.	Recognize the extent to which a culture's structures and values may oppress, marginalize, alienate, or create or enhance privilege and power						
b.	Gain sufficient self-awareness to eliminate the influence of personal biases and values in working with diverse groups						
c.	Recognize and communicate their understanding of the importance of difference in shaping life experiences						
d.	View themselves as learners and engage those with whom they work as informants						
EP 2.1.5 Advance Human Rights and Social and Economic Justice:							
a.	Understand forms and mechanisms of oppression and discrimination						
b.	Advocate for human rights and social and economic justice						
c.	Engage in practices that advance social and economic justice						
EP 2.1.6 Engage in Research-Informed Practice and Practice-Informed Research:							
a.	Use practice experience to inform scientific inquiry						
b.	Use research evidence to inform practice						

EP 2.1.7 Apply Knowledge of Human Behavior and the Social Environment:						
a. Utilize conceptual frameworks to guide the processes of assessment, intervention, and evaluation						
b. Critique and apply knowledge to understand person and environment						
EP 2.1.8 Engage in Policy Practice to Advance Social and Economic Well-Being and to Deliver Effective Social Work Services:						
a. Analyze, formulate, and advocate for policies that advance social well-being						
b. Collaborate with colleagues and clients for effective policy action						
EP 2.1.9 Respond to Contexts that Shape Practice:						
a. Continuously discover, appraise, and attend to changing locales, populations, scientific and technological developments, and emerging societal trends to provide relevant services						
b. Provide leadership in promoting sustainable changes in service delivery and practice to improve the quality of social services						
EP 2.1.10 Engage, Assess, Intervene, and Evaluate with Individuals, Families, Groups, Organizations and Communities:						
a. Substantively and affectively prepare for action with individuals, families, groups, organizations, and communities						
b. Use empathy and other interpersonal skills						
c. Develop a mutually agreed-on focus of work and desired outcomes						
d. Collect, organize, and interpret client data						
e. Assess client strengths and limitations						
f. Develop mutually agreed-on intervention goals and objectives						
g. Select appropriate intervention strategies						
h. Initiate actions to achieve organizational goals						
i. Implement prevention interventions that enhance client capacities						
j. Help clients resolve problems						
k. Negotiate, mediate, and advocate for clients						
l. Facilitate transitions and endings						
m. Critically analyze, monitor, and evaluate interventions						

Chapter 12
Culturally Competent Social Work Practice

Competencies/Practice Behaviors Exercise 12.1
Ethnic Sensitive Strategies

Focus Competencies or Practice Behaviors:
- EP 2.1.4a   Recognize the extent to which a culture's structures and values may oppress, marginalize, alienate, or create or enhance privilege and power
- EP 2.1.6b   Use research evidence to inform practice

Instructions:
A.   Locate one journal article, book, or professional paper which describes some aspect of social work practice with people of color. You might begin by looking at the bibliography for your text. In addition, you might wish to consult *Social Work Research and Abstracts, Psychlit,* or any computerized database available in your library.
B.   Read the article and identify one technique or strategy which the author(s) suggest will be helpful in working with people of color.
C.   Prepare a brief (one page) written summary of the technique and a critique of the author's research. In your review, answer these questions:

1.   Describe the approach suggested by the author(s).
2.   Does the author cite any research or study which supports his or her suggestions?
3.   Does the author mention the work of any other writers in her or his material?
4.   With which group(s) would this approach be most successful, according to the author(s)?
5.   Would you be comfortable using this approach? Why or why not?

D.   Briefly report on your findings in class. Be prepared to answer any questions from the instructor or other students.
E.   Turn your one-page paper in at the end of the class.

Competencies/Practice Behaviors Exercise 12.2
Ethnic Heritage

Focus Competencies or Practice Behaviors:
- EP 2.1.1b   Practice personal reflection and self-correction to assure continual professional development
- EP 2.1.4a   Recognize the extent to which a culture's structures and values may oppress, marginalize, alienate, or create or enhance privilege and power
- EP 2.1.4b   Gain sufficient self-awareness to eliminate the influence of personal biases and values in working with diverse groups
- EP 2.1.4c   Recognize and communicate their understanding of the importance of difference in shaping life experiences

Instructions:
A.   This exercise will identify several ways in which your life has been influenced by your cultural and ethnic heritage, and help you understand the importance of ethnic heritage in shaping behavior, beliefs, and perceptions.

189

1. List the ethnic groups with which you most identify. This might include German, Polish, Nigerian, Japanese, etc.

2. Identify the country(ies) from which your grandparents or great-grandparents came.

3. Record any religious orientation held by your great-grandparents, grandparents, parents, and you.

4. Look at the list you have produced. Which groups (ethnic, cultural, religious, and so on) have affected your development? Think about the messages which you have received from each of these groups. What are the behaviors, attitudes, beliefs, and values transmitted by these groups? To what extent are you in agreement with these? Which have you rejected and why? What advantages or benefits have you experienced because of your background? What disadvantages, if any, have you experienced?

5. In what ways might your own cultural heritage affect your work as a social worker? Is being aware of your heritage likely to enhance or detract from your ability to work with people from different groups? Why?

190

Competencies/Practice Behaviors Exercise 12.3
Tough Decisions

Focus Competencies or Practice Behaviors:
- EP 2.1.3   Apply critical thinking to inform and communicate professional judgments
- EP 2.1.4c   Recognize and communicate their understanding of the importance of difference in shaping life experiences

Instructions:
A.   Read the case situation and decide how to answer the questions which follow.

Case Situation #1

Mary Wong and Mary Perez have both applied for the Social Worker I position in your agency. Both have similar educational backgrounds, and neither has experience since they just graduated from the same B.S.W. program. Mary Wong, who is Chinese, and Mary Perez, who is Mexican-American, are both qualified for the position.

1.   If you were in a position to hire one of them, what further information would you need or like to have?

2.   If both are equally qualified, upon what would you base your decision?

Case Situation #2

Assume that Mary Wong is not Chinese, but is married to Richard Wong, who is.

1.   Does this change your decision-making process in any way? Why or why not?

191

Case Situation #3
Roberto and Ernesto Rivas have been picked up by the police for shoplifting. You are the social worker responsible for doing an initial assessment and either recommending information (non-court) intervention or referring them to juvenile court for a finding of delinquency.

1.   What information would you need before making a decision?

2.   Does the ethnic or cultural background of the clients make any difference in what you might do? Why or why not?

Case Situation #4
You are a school social worker. The teacher has referred to you a young Native American boy who she says is "too quiet" in class. According to the teacher, he speaks only when spoken to and rarely makes eye contact with her. She is concerned that he is having a problem relating to her and is afraid that his quietness will cause him academic problems eventually.

1.   What will you say to the teacher? Why?

2.   What will you say to the boy? Why?

Focus Competencies or Practice Behaviors:

- EP 2.1.3   Apply critical thinking to inform and communicate professional judgment
- EP 2.1.4a   Recognize the extent to which a culture's structures and values may oppress, marginalize, alienate, or create or enhance privilege and power
- EP 2.1.5a   Understand the forms and mechanisms of oppression and discrimination
- EP 2.1.10e Assess client strengths and limitations

Instructions:

A.   Before beginning this exercise, review the material in the text on culturally competent social work.

B.   Volunteers are needed to participate in a role play. Otherwise, your instructor will assign roles.

C.   Volunteers should seat themselves in front of the class where they can be observed easily.

D.   One person will play a client whose cultural background is different from the worker. The role play should continue for twenty to thirty minutes. Your instructor will indicate to the role players when it's time to stop.

> **The worker:** **Elise** is a white, female worker at Laconte County Human Services Department. Laconte County is in a Midwestern state with a strong base of farmers with Norwegian backgrounds. Most are second or third generation family farms.
>
> **The client:** **Mr. Guillermo Suente** is an eighty-five-year-old gentleman who is experiencing poor health. He has no money and has been in the United States illegally from Mexico for over thirty years. He has raised a family with his wife, Juanita, who passed away a year ago. Mr. Suente is accompanied by his oldest daughter, **Selena**. Mr. Suente speaks very little English and he doesn't want to be here. He has always believed in the curanderos (medicine men) for his well-being. Selena has forced Mr. Suente to come today and hopes that Elise can provide some direction to help her papa.

E.   During the role play, observers should take notes on the form shown below as they address the following questions:

> **Role Play Feedback Form**
>
> A.   Did the worker greet the client appropriately, keeping in mind cultural traditions? What was done well, and what could have been done differently?

B. Do you think the worker paid particular attention to the nonverbal communication of the client? Do you believe the eye contact was appropriate for this ethnic group? Was the interpretation difficult for Elise? Did she make eye contact with Mr. Suente, or was she paying too much attention to the daughter, who was translating?

C. Was there an appropriate amount of both open-ended and closed-ended questions?

D. Did the worker demonstrate interest in the client's traditions and customs?

E. What did you learn from this role-play regarding culturally competent social work?

194

Chapter 12 Competencies/Practice Behaviors Exercises Assessment:

Name: _____ **Date:** _____

Supervisor's Name: _____

Focus Competencies/Practice Behaviors:

- EP 2.1.1b   Practice personal reflection and self-correction to assure continual professional development
- EP 2.1.3   Apply critical thinking to inform and communicate professional judgments
- EP 2.1.4a   Recognize the extent to which a culture's structures and values may oppress, marginalize, alienate, or create or enhance privilege and power
- EP 2.1.4b   Gain sufficient self-awareness to eliminate the influence of personal biases and values in working with diverse groups
- EP 2.1.4c   Recognize and communicate their understanding of the importance of difference in shaping life experiences
- EP 2.1.5a   Understand forms and mechanisms of oppression and discrimination
- EP 2.1.6b   Use research evidence to inform practice
- EP 2.1.10e   Assess client strengths and limitations

Instructions:

A.   Evaluate your work or your partner's work in the Focus Competencies/Practice Behaviors by completing the Competencies/Practice Behaviors Assessment form below

B.   What other Competencies/Practice Behaviors did you use to complete these Exercises? Be sure to record them in your assessments

1.	I have attained this competency/practice behavior (in the range of 81 to 100%)
2.	I have largely attained this competency/practice behavior (in the range of 61 to 80%)
3.	I have partially attained this competency/practice behavior (in the range of 41 to 60%)
4.	I have made a little progress in attaining this competency/practice behavior (in the range of 21 to 40%)
5.	I have made almost no progress in attaining this competency/practice behavior (in the range of 0 to 20%)

EPAS 2008 Core Competencies & Core Practice Behaviors	Student Self Assessment						Evaluator Feedback
Student and Evaluator Assessment Scale and Comments	0	1	2	3	4	5	**Agree/Disagree/Comments**
EP 2.1.1 Identify as a Professional Social Worker and Conduct Oneself Accordingly:							
a. Advocate for client access to the services of social work							
b. Practice personal reflection and self-correction to assure continual professional development							
c. Attend to professional roles and boundaries							
d. Demonstrate professional demeanor in behavior, appearance, and communication							
e. Engage in career-long learning							
f. Use supervision and consultation							
EP 2.1.2 Apply Social Work Ethical Principles to Guide Professional Practice:							
a. Recognize and manage personal values in a way that allows professional values to guide practice							

195

b.	Make ethical decisions by applying NASW Code of Ethics and, as applicable, of the IFSW/IASSW Ethics in Social Work, Statement of Principles					
c.	Tolerate ambiguity in resolving ethical conflicts					
d.	Apply strategies of ethical reasoning to arrive at principled decisions					
EP 2.1.3 Apply Critical Thinking to Inform and Communicate Professional Judgments:						
a.	Distinguish, appraise, and integrate multiple sources of knowledge, including research-based knowledge and practice wisdom					
b.	Analyze models of assessment, prevention, intervention, and evaluation					
c.	Demonstrate effective oral and written communication in working with individuals, families, groups, organizations, communities, and colleagues					
EP 2.1.4 Engage Diversity and Difference in Practice:						
a.	Recognize the extent to which a culture's structures and values may oppress, marginalize, alienate, or create or enhance privilege and power					
b.	Gain sufficient self-awareness to eliminate the influence of personal biases and values in working with diverse groups					
c.	Recognize and communicate their understanding of the importance of difference in shaping life experiences					
d.	View themselves as learners and engage those with whom they work as informants					
EP 2.1.5 Advance Human Rights and Social and Economic Justice:						
a.	Understand forms and mechanisms of oppression and discrimination					
b.	Advocate for human rights and social and economic justice					
c.	Engage in practices that advance social and economic justice					
EP 2.1.6 Engage in Research-Informed Practice and Practice-Informed Research:						
a.	Use practice experience to inform scientific inquiry					
b.	Use research evidence to inform practice					
EP 2.1.7 Apply Knowledge of Human Behavior and the Social Environment:						
a.	Utilize conceptual frameworks to guide the processes of assessment, intervention, and evaluation					
b.	Critique and apply knowledge to understand person and environment					
EP 2.1.8 Engage in Policy Practice to Advance Social and Economic Well-Being and to Deliver Effective Social Work Services:						
a.	Analyze, formulate, and advocate for policies that advance social well-being					
b.	Collaborate with colleagues and clients for effective policy action					

EP 2.1.9 Respond to Contexts that Shape Practice:							
a. Continuously discover, appraise, and attend to changing locales, populations, scientific and technological developments, and emerging societal trends to provide relevant services							
b. Provide leadership in promoting sustainable changes in service delivery and practice to improve the quality of social services							
EP 2.1.10 Engage, Assess, Intervene, and Evaluate with Individuals, Families, Groups, Organizations and Communities:							
a. Substantively and affectively prepare for action with individuals, families, groups, organizations, and communities							
b. Use empathy and other interpersonal skills							
c. Develop a mutually agreed-on focus of work and desired outcomes							
d. Collect, organize, and interpret client data							
e. Assess client strengths and limitations							
f. Develop mutually agreed-on intervention goals and objectives							
g. Select appropriate intervention strategies							
h. Initiate actions to achieve organizational goals							
i. Implement prevention interventions that enhance client capacities							
j. Help clients resolve problems							
k. Negotiate, mediate, and advocate for clients							
l. Facilitate transitions and endings							
m. Critically analyze, monitor, and evaluate interventions							

Competencies/Practice Behaviors Exercise 13.1
Gender Relations Quiz

Focus Competencies or Practice Behaviors:
- EP 2.1.1b   Practice personal reflection and self-correction to assure continual professional development
- EP 2.1.2b   Make ethical decisions by applying standards of the NASW Code of Ethics and, as applicable, of the IFSW/IASSW Ethics in Social Work, Statement of Principles
- EP 2.1.4a   Recognize the extent to which a culture's structures and values may oppress, marginalize, alienate, or create or enhance privilege and power
- EP 2.1.4b   Gain sufficient self-awareness to eliminate the influence of personal biases and values in working with diverse groups
- EP 2.1.4c   Recognize and communicate their understanding of the importance of difference in shaping life experiences

Instructions:
A.   Complete the "Gender Relations Quiz" below. For each statement, check whether you agree or disagree. You must commit yourself to one answer or the other. Additionally, note briefly the reasons for your answers.

Gender Relations Quiz

a.   Employers should treat men and women equally in work settings.
         ☐ Agree   ☐ Disagree
Reason: _____
_____

b.   Men make better supervisors than women.
         ☐ Agree   ☐ Disagree
Reason: _____
_____

c.   Men make better leaders than women.
         ☐ Agree   ☐ Disagree
Reason: _____
_____

d.   A woman would probably not be elected president.
         ☐ Agree   ☐ Disagree
Reason: _____
_____

---

e.   Mothers of small children should remain at home to care for them.
       ☐ Agree   ☐ Disagree
       Reason: _____
       _____

f.   Women should automatically be granted several months leave of absence from paid employment when having a baby.
       ☐ Agree   ☐ Disagree
       Reason: _____
       _____

g.   Employers should continue paying such women full salary during their absences.
       ☐ Agree   ☐ Disagree
       Reason: _____
       _____

h.   In a heterosexual couple, a man should be the "head of the house."
       ☐ Agree   ☐ Disagree
       Reason: _____
       _____

i.   Among heterosexual couples, men generally are the "heads of the house."
       ☐ Agree   ☐ Disagree
       Reason: _____
       _____

j.   Women and men living together should share housework (for example, taking out the garbage, cleaning the bathroom, doing the laundry, washing dishes, cooking, grocery shopping, taking care of the children) equally.
       ☐ Agree   ☐ Disagree
       Reason: _____
       _____

k.   Women and men living together really do share housework equally.
       ☐ Agree   ☐ Disagree
       Reason: _____
       _____

l.   If you marry (or are married), you will share (or do share) housework equally with your spouse.
       ☐ Agree   ☐ Disagree
       Reason: _____
       _____

B.   Divide into groups of four to six persons. Discuss the Gender Quiz statements, your respective answers, and your rationales for each. After your discussion, a volunteer from each group will be asked to summarize the group's findings and ideas for the entire class.

C.   After approximately twenty minutes, each group's volunteer should present her or his summary. Then address with the entire class the following questions:

1.   Is power and opportunity distributed equally between genders? Why or why not?

2.   What are your own opinions and biases about these issues?

3.   How do these coincide with professional social work values and ethics?

4.   In those instances where you perceive inequities, what suggestions do you have to make changes?

5.   What can you *personally* do to bring about positive change?

Focus Competencies or Practice Behaviors:
- EP 2.1.1b   Practice personal reflection and self-correction to assure continual professional development
- EP 2.1.4a   Recognize the extent to which a culture's structures and values may oppress, marginalize, alienate, or create or enhance privilege and power
- EP 2.1.4b   Gain sufficient self-awareness to eliminate the influence of personal biases and values in working with diverse groups
- EP 2.1.4c   Recognize and communicate their understanding of the importance of difference in shaping life experiences
- EP 2.1.5a   Understand forms and mechanisms of oppression and discrimination

Instructions:
A.   Divide into small groups of four to six persons.
B.   Each group will theoretically have a total of $45,000 that it may allocate to any one of the client situations described below. You may only allocate the total amount to address one situation. Assume that any lesser (or divided) amount would be inadequate to meet the need and, therefore, would be useless.

Situation 1

Julia, age twenty-three, and her four young children are homeless. All the shelters are filled. She married at age seventeen and never worked outside of the home. She and her children had always been poor, her husband jumping from one low-paying, blue-collar job to another. Last month her husband told her he was sick of her and all of his responsibility. He abruptly left without telling her where he was going. Julia has no money at all. She also desperately needs food and clothing for her family. She has no access to relatives or other personal support systems who could help her. Additionally, to remove herself from her homeless situation permanently, she needs job training along with concurrent daycare.

Situation 2

Jeannette, age twenty-nine, was raped fourteen months ago and now has discovered she has AIDS. Her assailant has been apprehended and she has learned he is HIV-positive. Thus, she thinks he was the one who contaminated her. Her health has deteriorated rapidly. She desperately needs expensive health care including the new "cocktail drugs" which could help her keep at least some of the more severe diseases at bay. She had been a secretary. Her health problems no longer allow her to work. Nor does she have any health insurance. Her savings are completely depleted.

Situation 3

Danielle, age fifteen, has been on the streets for two years. She thinks she is cocaine and alcohol addicted. She ran away from home because her stepfather had been sexually abusing her since she was eleven. She couldn't stand it anymore. She needs both a home and an expensive rehabilitation program to survive.

Situation 4

Gertie, age thirty-seven, is a battered wife. The beatings are getting worse and worse. She literally doesn't know how long she can live in her battering environment. She is only one of about 150 battered women identified in the small Midwestern town. Counseling, day care, legal aid, and a place of respite for these women are desperately needed. However, a minimum of $40,000 is required to keep the shelter for them open another three months.

Situation 5

Ruth, age fifty-seven, has been divorced for twenty-three months. Her ex-husband, a businessman two years her senior, left her to run off with a twenty-six-year-old woman. He had an excellent and expensive lawyer. The state in which they lived did not treat divorced women very kindly. Additionally, her ex-husband was able to manipulate most of their assets so that they had become hidden and unavailable to her. She received half of the money from their house and $730 a month in alimony for two years. Their house had been beautiful, but their equity in it had been relatively little. As a result, she now has almost no money left and alimony is about to stop. Her ex-husband has spent thirty-five years establishing a career for himself. He is well off. However, Ruth had spent her life taking care of his home, entertaining his associates, and doing charity work for her community. She has no experience working outside of the home other than the minimum-wage job she has managed to get serving yogurt at a local frozen yogurt store. Her reserve of cash is almost gone. What she earns now will barely pay for her rent, let alone for her food, health care, and other needs. She has no idea about what she will do.

C. Take approximately fifteen minutes for discussion. A volunteer from each group should be prepared to share with the entire class the group's decision regarding how to spend the money.

D. Rejoin the entire class for a discussion which addresses the following questions:

1. What were your reasons for choosing the situation you did to allocate the resources?

2. To what extent did you find the experience frustrating and why?

3. Whose fault was it that each situation occurred?

4. Did you feel our society failed these people, and, if so, how?

5.   What aspects of policies, social programs, and laws contributed to these people's problems?

6.   Do you see aspects of sexism and oppression based on gender, and, if so, what are they?

7.   How do you think you'd feel if you were in a situation similar to each one described above?

Competencies/Practice Behaviors Exercise 13.3
Proposing Intervention Strategies for Women in Need

Focus Competencies or Practice Behaviors:
- EP 2.1.4a   Recognize the extent to which a culture's structures and values may oppress, marginalize, alienate, or create or enhance privilege and power
- EP 2.1.10g   Select appropriate intervention strategies

Instructions:
A.   Review once more the vignettes presented above in Exercise 13.2.
B.   Break up into small groups of four to six persons.
C.   For each vignette, the groups should establish an intervention alternative. Allow thirty minutes for this process.
D.   A volunteer from each group should explain the group's recommendation to the entire class. Vignettes should be addressed one at a time. Discussion should focus on which intervention alternatives are most doable and have the greatest potential for effectiveness.
E.   Review the definition of feminism. Discuss with the group the extent to which each alternative reflects feminist perspectives.

Competencies/Practice Behaviors Exercise 13.4
Confronting Sexual Harassment

Focus Competencies or Practice Behaviors:
- EP 2.1.4a   Recognize the extent to which a culture's structures and values may oppress, marginalize, alienate, or create or enhance privilege and power
- EP 2.1.10g   Select appropriate intervention strategies

Instructions:
A.   Review the material in the text concerning improving conditions in the workplace, especially that about sexual harassment.
B.   Read the following vignettes one at a time.

Vignette #1
Ann's boss states that if she doesn't go to bed with him, she won't make it through her six-month probationary period. She really needs the job. She knows she has the right to complain, but knows she would be labeled a troublemaker. The management would probably find a way to "let her go." They had done so with others before. She doesn't know what to do.

Vignette #2
Barbara's male supervisor likes to sneak up behind her and surprise her by putting his arms around her. This makes her feel very uncomfortable. However, he's responsible for scheduling her hours, evaluating her work performance, and giving her salary increases. She is terrified of confronting him.

Vignette #3
Lavinia really needs to get a good grade in a course she's taking with a male professor, Dr. Driven, in order to keep her scholarship and stay in school. So far, she has only achieved a grade of D+. When Lavinia goes to see Dr. Driven, he frequently touches her arm and pats her knee. He acts exceptionally friendly with her. Last Thursday Dr. Driven said he would "see what could be done about improving the grade" if Lavinia would start dating him. Lavinia feels trapped. She doesn't know what to do.

Vignette #4
One of the other financial assistance workers in the county social services department really annoys *Irene*. The man is constantly telling dirty jokes about women. Additionally, he likes to whistle at any woman under age twenty-five who passes his desk. His favorite phrase in life seems to be, "Wow, look at the big bozooms on that one!"

C.   After reading a vignette, take about ten minutes to answer the following questions:

1.   How does this situation fit the definition of sexual harassment?

2.   To what extent are the victim's feelings valid?

3.   How do you feel about this situation?

4.   What do you think the victim should do?

5.   What do you think you would do in this same situation?

Competencies/Practice Behaviors Exercise 13.5
Are You a Feminist?

Focus Competencies or Practice Behaviors:

- EP 2.1.1b   Practice personal reflection and self-correction to assure continual professional development
- EP 2.1.2a   Recognize and manage personal values in a way that allows professional values to guide practice
- EP 2.1.4a   Recognize the extent to which a culture's structures and values may oppress, marginalize, alienate, or create or enhance privilege and power
- EP 2.1.4b   Gain sufficient self-awareness to eliminate the influence of personal biases and values in working with diverse groups
- EP 2.1.4c   Recognize and communicate their understanding of the importance of difference in shaping life experiences
- EP 2.1.4d   View themselves as learners and engage those with whom they work as informants

Instructions:
A.   Review chapter 13, "Gender Sensitive Social Work Practice."
B.   Individually, read the questionnaire cited below and check "yes" or "no" for each question.

Questionnaire:
Are You a Feminist?

a.   Do you believe that women should have the same rights as men?
     ☐ Yes   ☐ No

b.   Do you believe that women should have the same access to jobs and social status as men?
     ☐ Yes   ☐ No

c.   Do you believe that women should *not* be discriminated against or *denied* opportunities and choices on the basis of their gender?
     ☐ Yes   ☐ No

d.   Do you believe that, ideally, both people's attitudes and behavior should reflect the equal treatment of women?
     ☐ Yes   ☐ No

e.   Do you think that many people need to become more educated about women's issues?
     ☐ Yes   ☐ No

f.   Would you be willing to advocate on behalf of women (for instance, for poor women or women who have been raped)?
     ☐ Yes   ☐ No

g.   Do you believe that both men and women have the right to their own individual differences (that is, of course, differences which don't harm other people)?
     ☐ Yes   ☐ No

h.   Do you think that our society is generally structured legally, socially, and economically by and for men instead of women? (This last question is probably the most difficult, and perhaps the most painful, to answer.)
     ☐ Yes   ☐ No

C.   Count the number of times you answered "yes" to the eight questions.

D.   Focus specifically on the definition of feminism which includes the following concepts:
     a.   Philosophy of equality.
     b.   Involvement of both attitudes and actions.
     c.   Involvement of all aspects of life.
     d.   Necessity of providing education and advocacy.
     e.   Appreciation of individual differences.

E.   Discuss the following questions and issues:

1.   Are you or are you not a feminist? Explain why or why not.

2.   How would you define feminism?

3.   What negative images does feminism conjure up for many people?

4.   To what extent do feminist principles contradict or coincide with professional social work values?

Competencies/Practice Behaviors Exercise 13.6
Role-Play: Confronting Sexual Harassment

Focus Competencies or Practice Behaviors:
- EP 2.1.2b   Make ethical decisions by applying standards of the NASW Code of Ethics and, as applicable, of the IFSW/IASSW Ethics in Social Work, Statement of Principles
- EP 2.1.4a   Recognize the extent to which a culture's structures and values may oppress, marginalize, alienate, or create or enhance privilege and power
- EP 2.1.5a   Understand forms and mechanisms of oppression and discrimination
- EP 2.1.10g   Select appropriate intervention strategies

Instructions:
A.   Review the material in the text concerning improving conditions in the workplace, especially that about sexual harassment.
B.   Role play the following vignette (not too vividly). The pressure is on Brazilla, obviously, to give Lavinia the correct advice.

Vignette #1

Lavinia really needs to get a good grade in a course she's taking with a male professor, Dr. Driven, in order to keep her scholarship and stay in school. So far, she has only achieved a grade of D+. When Lavinia goes to see Dr. Driven, he frequently touches her arm and pats her knee. He acts exceptionally friendly with her. Last Thursday Dr. Driven said he would "see what could be done about improving the grade" if Lavinia would start dating him. Lavinia feels trapped. She doesn't know what to do.

She decides to talk to a friend of hers, Brazilla, who is a social work student. Brazilla has just had a class on sexual harassment and explains to Lavinia what she needs to do.

Role Play Feedback Form

A.   How do you think Brazilla did advising her friend Lavinia? Be specific.

B.   Do you see any weaknesses or areas in which improvement would be helpful? (Specific suggestions for how to improve are beneficial.)

C.   What do you think will ultimately be the outcome of this situation?

D.   Do you have any additional thoughts or comments?

Chapter 13 Competencies/Practice Behaviors Exercises Assessment:

Name: _____ **Date:** _____
Supervisor's Name: _____

Focus Competencies/Practice Behaviors:

- EP 2.1.1b   Practice personal reflection and self-correction to assure continual professional development
- EP 2.1.2a   Recognize and manage personal values in a way that allows professional values to guide practice
- EP 2.1.2b   Make ethical decisions by applying standards of the NASW Code of Ethics and, as applicable, of the IFSW/IASSW Ethics in Social Work, Statement of Principles
- EP 2.1.4a   Recognize the extent to which a culture's structures and values may oppress, marginalize, alienate, or create or enhance privilege and power
- EP 2.1.4b   Gain sufficient self-awareness to eliminate the influence of personal biases and values in working with diverse groups
- EP 2.1.4c   Recognize and communicate their understanding of the importance of difference in shaping life experiences
- EP 2.1.4d   View themselves as learners and engage those with whom they work as informants
- EP 2.1.5a   Understand forms and mechanisms of oppression and discrimination
- EP 2.1.10g   Select appropriate intervention strategies

Instructions:

A.   Evaluate your work or your partner's work in the Focus Competencies/Practice Behaviors by completing the Competencies/Practice Behaviors Assessment form below
B.   What other Competencies/Practice Behaviors did you use to complete these Exercises? Be sure to record them in your assessments

1.	I have attained this competency/practice behavior (in the range of 81 to 100%)
2.	I have largely attained this competency/practice behavior (in the range of 61 to 80%)
3.	I have partially attained this competency/practice behavior (in the range of 41 to 60%)
4.	I have made a little progress in attaining this competency/practice behavior (in the range of 21 to 40%)
5.	I have made almost no progress in attaining this competency/practice behavior (in the range of 0 to 20%)

EPAS 2008 Core Competencies & Core Practice Behaviors			Student Self Assessment					Evaluator Feedback
Student and Evaluator Assessment Scale and Comments	**0**	**1**	**2**	**3**	**4**	**5**	**Agree/Disagree/Comments**	
EP 2.1.1 Identify as a Professional Social Worker and Conduct Oneself Accordingly:								
a. Advocate for client access to the services of social work								
b. Practice personal reflection and self-correction to assure continual professional development								
c. Attend to professional roles and boundaries								
d. Demonstrate professional demeanor in behavior, appearance, and communication								
e. Engage in career-long learning								
f. Use supervision and consultation								

EP 2.1.2 Apply Social Work Ethical Principles to Guide Professional Practice:							
a. Recognize and manage personal values in a way that allows professional values to guide practice							
b. Make ethical decisions by applying NASW Code of Ethics and, as applicable, of the IFSW/IASSW Ethics in Social Work, Statement of Principles							
c. Tolerate ambiguity in resolving ethical conflicts							
d. Apply strategies of ethical reasoning to arrive at principled decisions							
EP 2.1.3 Apply Critical Thinking to Inform and Communicate Professional Judgments:							
a. Distinguish, appraise, and integrate multiple sources of knowledge, including research-based knowledge and practice wisdom							
b. Analyze models of assessment, prevention, intervention, and evaluation							
c. Demonstrate effective oral and written communication in working with individuals, families, groups, organizations, communities, and colleagues							
EP 2.1.4 Engage Diversity and Difference in Practice:							
a. Recognize the extent to which a culture's structures and values may oppress, marginalize, alienate, or create or enhance privilege and power							
b. Gain sufficient self-awareness to eliminate the influence of personal biases and values in working with diverse groups							
c. Recognize and communicate their understanding of the importance of difference in shaping life experiences							
d. View themselves as learners and engage those with whom they work as informants							
EP 2.1.5 Advance Human Rights and Social and Economic Justice:							
a. Understand forms and mechanisms of oppression and discrimination							
b. Advocate for human rights and social and economic justice							
c. Engage in practices that advance social and economic justice							
EP 2.1.6 Engage in Research-Informed Practice and Practice-Informed Research:							
a. Use practice experience to inform scientific inquiry							
b. Use research evidence to inform practice							
EP 2.1.7 Apply Knowledge of Human Behavior and the Social Environment:							
a. Utilize conceptual frameworks to guide the processes of assessment, intervention, and evaluation							
b. Critique and apply knowledge to understand person and environment							

EP 2.1.8 Engage in Policy Practice to Advance Social and Economic Well-Being and to Deliver Effective Social Work Services:								
a. Analyze, formulate, and advocate for policies that advance social well-being								
b. Collaborate with colleagues and clients for effective policy action								
EP 2.1.9 Respond to Contexts that Shape Practice:								
a. Continuously discover, appraise, and attend to changing locales, populations, scientific and technological developments, and emerging societal trends to provide relevant services								
b. Provide leadership in promoting sustainable changes in service delivery and practice to improve the quality of social services								
EP 2.1.10 Engage, Assess, Intervene, and Evaluate with Individuals, Families, Groups, Organizations and Communities:								
a. Substantively and affectively prepare for action with individuals, families, groups, organizations, and communities								
b. Use empathy and other interpersonal skills								
c. Develop a mutually agreed-on focus of work and desired outcomes								
d. Collect, organize, and interpret client data								
e. Assess client strengths and limitations								
f. Develop mutually agreed-on intervention goals and objectives								
g. Select appropriate intervention strategies								
h. Initiate actions to achieve organizational goals								
i. Implement prevention interventions that enhance client capacities								
j. Help clients resolve problems								
k. Negotiate, mediate, and advocate for clients								
l. Facilitate transitions and endings								
m. Critically analyze, monitor, and evaluate interventions								

Chapter 14
Advocacy

Competencies/Practice Behaviors Exercise 14.1
Advocating for Renters

Focus Competencies or Practice Behaviors:
- EP 2.1.3   Apply critical thinking to inform and communicate professional judgments
- EP 2.1.5b   Advocate for human rights and social and economic justice
- EP 2.1.10d Collect, organize, and interpret client data
- EP 2.1.10f Develop mutually agreed-on intervention goals and objectives
- EP 2.1.10g Select appropriate intervention strategies

Instructions:
A.   Read the case situation and answer the questions.

Case Situation

The student residents of the Littlejake House were angry. The owner, Dwight Cackle, had taken advantage of Christmas break and began to remodel their apartments without informing them of his intentions. Cackle, hoping to increase his income, was combining an entry hall with portions of the original apartments to create another two apartments. His plan called for shaving three feet off the rooms on either side of the hallway and adding it to the hallway space. The diagram below shows his plan.

     The new apartments affect all the residents, who will each lose three feet from the end of their apartments. They will also lose the second exit since all apartments had two exits, one to the hallway and one to the outside. To make matters worse, he has turned off the water in the building since he says he has to do this to work on the new apartments. As a consequence, residents have no water, cannot use the bathrooms, and must listen to the pounding as work on the apartments continues. They have complained to Mr. Cackle, who has told them they're just complainers and he has no intention of stopping work on his project.

     As the ombudsman for the student housing office, you have often heard complaints about Mr. Cackle's actions toward tenants, including refusing to return security deposits, not following terms of the lease, and generally abusing residents of his apartments. Now the tenants have come to you for help. You must decide what you can do to assist them.

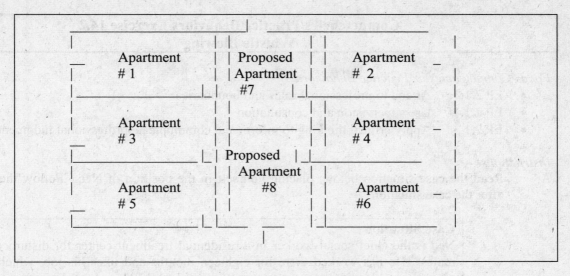

1. Which of the problems appear most serious to you? Why?

2. What information about the tenants would you like to have before attempting to help them?

3. List all possible sources of power available to you and the tenants.

4. What information about Mr. Cackle would help you assess his willingness to respond to your advocacy efforts?

5. What steps would you take to bring about change in this situation?

Focus Competencies or Practice Behaviors:
- EP 2.1.1c   Attend to professional roles and boundaries
- EP 2.1.1f   Use supervision and consultation
- EP 2.1.3   Apply critical thinking to inform and communicate professional judgments

Instructions:

A.   Read the case situation below, placing yourself in the position of Ned. Follow the steps listed after the case situation.

> **Case Situation**
> Ned is the chief social worker in a residential treatment center for disturbed adolescent males. He has worked there for eighteen months and likes his job, which consists of planning and leading treatment groups for residents of the center, designing entertainment such as sporting events, dances, and extracurricular activities, and supervising cottage parents who provide day-to-day supervision for the adolescents. In a conversation with a cottage parent, Ned hears an allegation that the treatment center director is pocketing financial donations to the center and diverting other resources to his own use. The cottage parent says this has been going on for a long time and he thought everybody knew about it. You indicate you knew nothing about this.

1.   If you were Ned, what would you say to the cottage parent who is your subordinate?

2.   Would you take any steps to determine whether this allegation is true? If so, what steps would you take?

3.   If you determined that the allegations were true, what possible steps (if any) might you take?

4.   For each possible step, list the advantages and risks involved.

5.   Which of the options would you be most likely to pursue? Why?

Competencies/Practice Behaviors Exercise 14.3
Persuasion

Focus Competencies or Practice Behaviors:
- EP 2.1.1d   Demonstrate professional demeanor in behavior, appearance, and communication
- EP 2.1.3   Apply critical thinking to inform and communicate professional judgments
- EP 2.1.3c   Demonstrate effective oral and written communication in working with individuals, families, groups, organizations, communities, and colleagues

Instructions:
A.   Review the section of the chapter describing the guidelines for persuasion.
B.   Read the case illustration and answer the questions.

> **Case Situation**
> Naomi Grunge was livid. "You don't care why I'm here or whether my client is in need or not. You have no right!" she shouted at Don Nedlin, Income Maintenance worker for Ashford County Human Services. "My client is entitled to lots of things and you have no basis for denying her," she continued. "What exactly are you asking for?" he said. "I want all my client is entitled to," said Naomi. Don started to respond by reciting the regulations he had to work with. "No!   I want none of that crap about regulations. You give my client everything she's supposed to get or else." At that point Don escorted Naomi to the front door of the agency, abruptly turned, and walked back to his office, locking the door behind him as he entered.

1. Which of the eight guidelines on persuading others did Naomi violate?

2. What effect did Naomi's shouting likely have on the person she was trying to persuade?

3. Was the "or else" threat a credible one? Why or why not?

4. Assume that you are a friend of Naomi's and that she would listen to you. What advice would you give her about how to handle this situation?

Focus Competencies or Practice Behaviors:

- EP 2.1.1a   Advocate for client access to the services of social work
- EP 2.1.1d   Demonstrate professional demeanor in behavior, appearance, and communication
- EP 2.1.2a   Recognize and manage personal values in a way that allows professional values to guide practice
- EP 2.1.3   Apply critical thinking to inform and communicate professional judgments
- EP 2.1.8b   Collaborate with colleagues and clients for effective policy action
- EP 2.1.10k Negotiate, mediate, and advocate for clients

Instructions:

A.   Review the information in the text regarding legislative advocacy.

B.   Read the situation below and assign people to the roles described. More people can participate than those stated. It is a public hearing. Stand up and be heard.

C.   The class can spend a few minutes with the volunteers who have assumed the listed roles. Everyone can join in the fun.

D.   Role-play the following situation and complete the questions below.

The Situation:

      A bill has been proposed to restrict access to reproductive health services such as Planned Parenthood. This agency provides information, contraception, counseling, and physical examinations, all directed at helping people (usually women) gain control over their own reproduction. Services are usually provided on a sliding-fee scale. This means that fees are based on how much people can pay. Poorer people pay less than richer people.

      Legislation limiting access might incorporate requirements such as forcing women under age 18 to provide written parental permission before they can receive any services. Along with this, they are proposing to deny state and federal funding if agency staff discuss abortion as a possible alternative to unwanted pregnancy.

      This proposed legislation is under Senate committee consideration. Opponents of this proposed bill have lobbied committee members, and a public hearing has been set to listen to all who wish to speak on the bill under consideration.

Roles at this Public Hearing:

The Coordinator, Corrine Clewso, "Corki" has the daunting position of keeping things rolling along and making sure that everybody who wants to voice his or her opinion is heard.

Committee member: Senator Spencer Claptrap, "Clapper" as he likes to be called, is all for this bill. He has stated many times that it is a sin to use contraception, and the mere word "abortion" turns him into a raving maniac. In private, he applauds the guys who shoot the abortion doctors. He believes his seat in the Senate is bought and paid for, so he is not worried about what these "peasants" have to say.

Committee member: Senator Loquacia Wordsmith is also at the public meeting because she feels strongly that this legislation should be buried somewhere the "sun don't shine."—preferably with Clapper right along with it. She welcomes this public hearing and has marshaled quite a few people who will speak against this bill.

217

> **Speaker: Sophia, is a social worker** at a nearby Planned Parenthood agency. Obviously she is against this legislation and has come prepared with lots and lots of statistics from her agency regarding how this legislation would adversely affect her clients.
>
> **Speaker: Adolf Stiller** is a member of the community and is very much for this legislation and is one of the original developers of the draft bill. He is sick and tired of all these losers and welfare queens having one baby after another, but thinks that the only way to stop this is abstinence. What is becoming of this younger generation anyway— with their loose morals.
>
> **Speaker: Stu Sensible** is a member of the City Council and really doesn't like the restrictions of this bill, but is willing to listen to all sides.
>
> **Speaker: May Happyflower** is another member of the community who just wants everybody to get along and doesn't see what the big deal is anyway. Why can't we all hold hands and sing "kumbaya". She likes the fact there are cookies and coffee and makes sure that all have some— to the extent that she is somewhat disruptive to the meeting.

1. Were you comfortable with this whole process? If you were a speaker, did you think you were able to make your point successfully? What could you have done differently?

2. Do you think this was an accurate portrayal of a public hearing? Why or why not?

3. Does legislative advocacy seem like something that would appeal to you when you become a social worker? Why or why not?

Chapter 14 Competencies/Practice Behaviors Exercises Assessment:

Name: _____ **Date:** _____

Supervisor's Name: _____

Focus Competencies/Practice Behaviors:

- EP 2.1.1a   Advocate for client access to the services of social work
- EP 2.1.1c   Attend to professional roles and boundaries
- EP 2.1.1d   Demonstrate professional demeanor in behavior, appearance, and communication
- EP 2.1.1f   Use supervision and consultation
- EP 2.1.2a   Recognize and manage personal values in a way that allows professional values to guide practice
- EP 2.1.3   Apply critical thinking to inform and communicate professional judgments
- EP 2.1.3c   Demonstrate effective oral and written communication in working with individuals, families, groups, organizations, communities, and colleagues
- EP 2.1.5b   Advocate for human rights and social and economic justice
- EP 2.1.8b   Collaborate with colleagues and clients for effective policy action
- EP 2.1.10g   Select appropriate intervention strategies
- EP 2.1.10d   Collect, organize, and interpret client data
- EP 2.1.10f   Develop mutually agreed-on intervention goals and objectives
- EP 2.1.10g   Select appropriate intervention strategies
- EP 2.1.10k   Negotiate, mediate, and advocate for clients

Instructions:

A.   Evaluate your work or your partner's work in the Focus Competencies/Practice Behaviors by completing the Competencies/Practice Behaviors Assessment form below

B.   What other Competencies/Practice Behaviors did you use to complete these Exercises? Be sure to record them in your assessments

1.	I have attained this competency/practice behavior (in the range of 81 to 100%)
2.	I have largely attained this competency/practice behavior (in the range of 61 to 80%)
3.	I have partially attained this competency/practice behavior (in the range of 41 to 60%)
4.	I have made a little progress in attaining this competency/practice behavior (in the range of 21 to 40%)
5.	I have made almost no progress in attaining this competency/practice behavior (in the range of 0 to 20%)

EPAS 2008 Core Competencies & Core Practice Behaviors							Student Self Assessment	Evaluator Feedback
Student and Evaluator Assessment Scale and Comments	0	1	2	3	4	5	**Agree/Disagree/Comments**
EP 2.1.1 Identify as a Professional Social Worker and Conduct Oneself Accordingly:								
a. Advocate for client access to the services of social work								
b. Practice personal reflection and self-correction to assure continual professional development								
c. Attend to professional roles and boundaries								
d. Demonstrate professional demeanor in behavior, appearance, and communication								
e. Engage in career-long learning								
f. Use supervision and consultation								

EP 2.1.2 Apply Social Work Ethical Principles to Guide Professional Practice:							
a.	Recognize and manage personal values in a way that allows professional values to guide practice						
b.	Make ethical decisions by applying NASW Code of Ethics and, as applicable, of the IFSW/IASSW Ethics in Social Work, Statement of Principles						
c.	Tolerate ambiguity in resolving ethical conflicts						
d.	Apply strategies of ethical reasoning to arrive at principled decisions						
EP 2.1.3 Apply Critical Thinking to Inform and Communicate Professional Judgments:							
a.	Distinguish, appraise, and integrate multiple sources of knowledge, including research-based knowledge and practice wisdom						
b.	Analyze models of assessment, prevention, intervention, and evaluation						
c.	Demonstrate effective oral and written communication in working with individuals, families, groups, organizations, communities, and colleagues						
EP 2.1.4 Engage Diversity and Difference in Practice:							
a.	Recognize the extent to which a culture's structures and values may oppress, marginalize, alienate, or create or enhance privilege and power						
b.	Gain sufficient self-awareness to eliminate the influence of personal biases and values in working with diverse groups						
c.	Recognize and communicate their understanding of the importance of difference in shaping life experiences						
d.	View themselves as learners and engage those with whom they work as informants						
EP 2.1.5 Advance Human Rights and Social and Economic Justice:							
a.	Understand forms and mechanisms of oppression and discrimination						
b.	Advocate for human rights and social and economic justice						
c.	Engage in practices that advance social and economic justice						
EP 2.1.6 Engage in Research-Informed Practice and Practice-Informed Research:							
a.	Use practice experience to inform scientific inquiry						
b.	Use research evidence to inform practice						
EP 2.1.7 Apply Knowledge of Human Behavior and the Social Environment:							
a.	Utilize conceptual frameworks to guide the processes of assessment, intervention, and evaluation						
b.	Critique and apply knowledge to understand person and environment						

EP 2.1.8 Engage in Policy Practice to Advance Social and Economic Well-Being and to Deliver Effective Social Work Services:							
a.	Analyze, formulate, and advocate for policies that advance social well-being						
b.	Collaborate with colleagues and clients for effective policy action						
EP 2.1.9 Respond to Contexts that Shape Practice:							
a.	Continuously discover, appraise, and attend to changing locales, populations, scientific and technological developments, and emerging societal trends to provide relevant services						
b.	Provide leadership in promoting sustainable changes in service delivery and practice to improve the quality of social services						
EP 2.1.10 Engage, Assess, Intervene, and Evaluate with Individuals, Families, Groups, Organizations and Communities:							
a.	Substantively and affectively prepare for action with individuals, families, groups, organizations, and communities						
b.	Use empathy and other interpersonal skills						
c.	Develop a mutually agreed-on focus of work and desired outcomes						
d.	Collect, organize, and interpret client data						
e.	Assess client strengths and limitations						
f.	Develop mutually agreed-on intervention goals and objectives						
g.	Select appropriate intervention strategies						
h.	Initiate actions to achieve organizational goals						
i.	Implement prevention interventions that enhance client capacities						
j.	Help clients resolve problems						
k.	Negotiate, mediate, and advocate for clients						
l.	Facilitate transitions and endings						
m.	Critically analyze, monitor, and evaluate interventions						

Competencies/Practice Behaviors Exercise 15.1
Mrs. Darwin

Focus Competencies or Practice Behaviors:

- EP 2.1.1c   Attend to professional roles and boundaries
- EP 2.1.3   Apply critical thinking to inform and communicate professional judgments
- EP 2.1.10f   Develop mutually agreed-on intervention goals and objectives
- EP 2.1.10g   Select appropriate intervention strategies

Instructions:

A.   Read the case situation below.

Case Situation

Mr. B. Darwin arrived at the trauma center after suffering a heart attack on the interstate highway. Attempts to revive him failed and the emergency room physician was about to talk to his wife. The Darwins, both in their late sixties, had apparently been traveling through the state on the way to visit relatives.

Mary Ann accompanied the doctor to the trauma center waiting room where they met Mrs. Darwin. A petite woman not even five feet tall, Mrs. Darwin looked very weary. The crumpled handkerchief in her hand was damp from tears. The doctor first introduced herself and Mary Ann. Mary Ann then sat next to Mrs. Darwin.

"Is he dead?" Mrs. Darwin asked quietly. The doctor slowly nodded his head and responded, "Yes, he is."

Mrs. Darwin put her head in her hands and cried softly for a minute. She raised her head and asked, "What am I going to do now?"

Mary Ann said that she knew this must be a terrible time for Mrs. Darwin and she offered to do everything she could to help her. She invited Mrs. Darwin to come to the social work office. As the doctor departed, Mary Ann reached out her hand and helped Mrs. Darwin to her feet. Together they took the elevator to Mary Ann's office.

Mary Ann again expressed her sensitivity to Mrs. Darwin's situation and asked her if there was anything that she (Mary Ann) could do. Slowly, Mrs. Darwin described the events of the day that preceded the death of her husband. In a few minutes, Mary Ann discovered the following information.

The Darwins were residents of Wisconsin traveling through Minnesota to visit relatives in Iowa. They had car trouble about fifteen miles from the hospital. When Mr. Darwin got out to check on the car, he fell to the ground. A passing trucker radioed a nearby highway patrol officer, and together they attempted cardiopulmonary resuscitation. Shortly, an ambulance arrived and transported Mr. Darwin to the hospital. The highway patrol officer brought Mrs. Darwin to the hospital with their pet, a small dog. Mrs. Darwin said the car was still on the side of the highway and contained a large load of frozen meat in the trunk. It was to be a gift to her daughter in Iowa, she explained. As they talked, Mary Ann began to make mental notes of the tasks ahead. She also learned a little about Mrs. Darwin. This would prove helpful as they worked together to resolve the woman's concerns.

B.   Answer the following questions:

1.   Prepare a list of tasks that must be completed in order to assist this client.

2.   Prioritize the tasks from most important to least important.

3.   Identify possible community resources to which the client might be referred.

Competencies/Practice Behaviors Exercise 15.2
Knowing Your Own Resources

Focus Competencies or Practice Behaviors:
  • EP 2.1.10e   Assess client strengths and limitations

Instructions:
A.   Read each of the "Need statements" below and list three resources that you could reasonably count on to assist you.

Needs Statements

a. Your car just quit working and you have a doctor's appointment in one hour.

Resource: _____

_____

b. You are sick and need a prescription picked up at the pharmacy.

Resource: _____

_____

c. You must pay your tuition of $1,000 by tomorrow morning or your enrollment in classes for this semester will be cancelled.

Resource: _____

_____

_____

d. You need a pair of dress slacks for a job interview and don't want to have to buy one.

Resource: _____

_____

e. You need a special book for your social work class tomorrow. The book costs $50. You have only $5 but your part-time job will pay you $75 in one week.

Resource: _____

_____

f. You have a job interview and need three letters of reference by tomorrow evening.

Resource: _____

_____

g. You need a haircut or perm by 5:00 p.m. today but have no money.

Resource: _____

_____

h. You have a date tomorrow night and no transportation. You definitely need a car to drive.

Resource: _____

_____

i. You have a chance for a part-time job that pays rather well, but you need to borrow a rake, hoe, and lawnmower.

Resource: _____

_____

j. You have nothing to eat in the house and have no money.

Resource: _____

_____

_____

k.   Your computer printer just quit in the middle of your final social work paper, which is due by noon tomorrow.

Resource: _____

_____

l.   You are very sick, don't have a local physician, and don't know what to do.

Resource: _____

_____

m.   Your favorite friend of the opposite sex just broke up with you and you need to talk to someone.

Resource: _____

_____

_____

Competencies/Practice Behaviors Exercise 15.3
Community Resources

Focus Competencies or Practice Behaviors:
- EP 2.1.10e   Assess client strengths and limitations
- EP 2.1.10f   Develop mutually agreed-on intervention goals and objectives

Instructions:
A.   Select two of the client situations listed below.
B.   Using any existing community resource directories, services, or telephone books, locate at least one resource for each of the client situations.
C.   List the resource under the problem situation.

Client Situations

a.   Twenty-two-year-old single mother of two children (ages one and three) has just lost her job and has no savings, no family, and no income.

Resource: _____

b.   Sixty-eight-year-old man being discharged from hospital to his own home needs a hospital-type bed provided at no charge.

Resource: _____

c.   Child has a serious vision disorder and needs corrective surgery. His parents are poor but not on welfare.

Resource: _____

d.   Father of six children has just lost his job and needs help locating another.

Resource: _____

e.   Homeless family just arrived in town and needs shelter for tonight and tomorrow night.

Resource: _____

f.   Child dying of cancer wants to go to Disney World before he dies.

Resource: _____

g. Tenant needs legal advice on whether her landlord can evict her for reporting him to the health department for bug infestation.
Resource: _____

h. Woman battered by her husband needs emergency shelter for herself and her five children.
Resource: _____

i. Alcoholic client needs to know meeting place and time of nearest Alcoholic Anonymous group.
Resource: _____

j. Child burn victim needs reconstructive surgery and parents have no money.
Resource: _____

k. Suicidal client needs to talk with someone immediately.
Resource: _____

Competencies/Practice Behaviors Exercise 15.4
Role-Play: Evaluating Interventions

Focus Competencies or Practice Behaviors:
- EP 2.1.10m   Critically analyze, monitor, and evaluate interventions

Instructions:
A.   You are the lead social worker in an agency team charged with ensuring that each intervention or resource selected to help a client has an evaluation component. The other three team members are social workers in your unit and will share responsibility for identifying appropriate evaluation methods. The lead social worker will report the group's decision to the unit supervisor.

B.   Select three of the client situations listed in Exercise 15.3 above.

1.   For each situation selected, identify at least two evaluation methods

2. As a group, discuss each method and select the one that seems most appropriate given the situation. Provide at least one reason why you selected a particular method.

Chapter 15 Competencies/Practice Behaviors Exercises Assessment:

Name: _____ Date: _____

Supervisor's Name: _____

Focus Competencies/Practice Behaviors:
- EP 2.1.1c   Attend to professional roles and boundaries
- EP 2.1.3   Apply critical thinking to inform and communicate professional judgments
- EP 2.1.10e   Assess client strengths and limitations
- EP 2.1.10f   Develop mutually agreed-on intervention goals and objectives
- EP 2.1.10g   Select appropriate intervention strategies
- EP 2.1.10m   Critically analyze, monitor, and evaluate interventions

Instructions:

A.   Evaluate your work or your partner's work in the Focus Competencies/Practice Behaviors by completing the Competencies/Practice Behaviors Assessment form below

B.   What other Competencies/Practice Behaviors did you use to complete these Exercises? Be sure to record them in your assessments

1.	I have attained this competency/practice behavior (in the range of 81 to 100%)
2.	I have largely attained this competency/practice behavior (in the range of 61 to 80%)
3.	I have partially attained this competency/practice behavior (in the range of 41 to 60%)
4.	I have made a little progress in attaining this competency/practice behavior (in the range of 21 to 40%)
5.	I have made almost no progress in attaining this competency/practice behavior (in the range of 0 to 20%)

EPAS 2008 Core Competencies & Core Practice Behaviors			Student Self Assessment					Evaluator Feedback
Student and Evaluator Assessment Scale and Comments	0	1	2	3	4	5		**Agree/Disagree/Comments**
EP 2.1.1 Identify as a Professional Social Worker and Conduct Oneself Accordingly:								
a. Advocate for client access to the services of social work								
b. Practice personal reflection and self-correction to assure continual professional development								
c. Attend to professional roles and boundaries								
d. Demonstrate professional demeanor in behavior, appearance, and communication								
e. Engage in career-long learning								
f. Use supervision and consultation								
EP 2.1.2 Apply Social Work Ethical Principles to Guide Professional Practice:								
a. Recognize and manage personal values in a way that allows professional values to guide practice								
b. Make ethical decisions by applying NASW Code of Ethics and, as applicable, of the IFSW/IASSW Ethics in Social Work, Statement of Principles								
c. Tolerate ambiguity in resolving ethical conflicts								
d. Apply strategies of ethical reasoning to arrive at principled decisions								

EP 2.1.3 Apply Critical Thinking to Inform and Communicate Professional Judgments:							
a. Distinguish, appraise, and integrate multiple sources of knowledge, including research-based knowledge and practice wisdom							
b. Analyze models of assessment, prevention, intervention, and evaluation							
c. Demonstrate effective oral and written communication in working with individuals, families, groups, organizations, communities, and colleagues							
EP 2.1.4 Engage Diversity and Difference in Practice:							
a. Recognize the extent to which a culture's structures and values may oppress, marginalize, alienate, or create or enhance privilege and power							
b. Gain sufficient self-awareness to eliminate the influence of personal biases and values in working with diverse groups							
c. Recognize and communicate their understanding of the importance of difference in shaping life experiences							
d. View themselves as learners and engage those with whom they work as informants							
EP 2.1.5 Advance Human Rights and Social and Economic Justice:							
a. Understand forms and mechanisms of oppression and discrimination							
b. Advocate for human rights and social and economic justice							
c. Engage in practices that advance social and economic justice							
EP 2.1.6 Engage in Research-Informed Practice and Practice-Informed Research:							
a. Use practice experience to inform scientific inquiry							
b. Use research evidence to inform practice							
EP 2.1.7 Apply Knowledge of Human Behavior and the Social Environment:							
a. Utilize conceptual frameworks to guide the processes of assessment, intervention, and evaluation							
b. Critique and apply knowledge to understand person and environment							
EP 2.1.8 Engage in Policy Practice to Advance Social and Economic Well-Being and to Deliver Effective Social Work Services:							
a. Analyze, formulate, and advocate for policies that advance social well-being							
b. Collaborate with colleagues and clients for effective policy action							
EP 2.1.9 Respond to Contexts that Shape Practice:							
a. Continuously discover, appraise, and attend to changing locales, populations, scientific and technological developments, and emerging societal trends to provide relevant services							

b.	Provide leadership in promoting sustainable changes in service delivery and practice to improve the quality of social services						
EP 2.1.10 Engage, Assess, Intervene, and Evaluate with Individuals, Families, Groups, Organizations and Communities:							
a.	Substantively and affectively prepare for action with individuals, families, groups, organizations, and communities						
b.	Use empathy and other interpersonal skills						
c.	Develop a mutually agreed-on focus of work and desired outcomes						
d.	Collect, organize, and interpret client data						
e.	Assess client strengths and limitations						
f.	Develop mutually agreed-on intervention goals and objectives						
g.	Select appropriate intervention strategies						
h.	Initiate actions to achieve organizational goals						
i.	Implement prevention interventions that enhance client capacities						
j.	Help clients resolve problems						
k.	Negotiate, mediate, and advocate for clients						
l.	Facilitate transitions and endings						
m.	Critically analyze, monitor, and evaluate interventions						

Chapter 16
Recording in Generalist Social Work Practice

Competencies/Practice Behaviors Exercise 16.1
Filling Out a Face Sheet

Focus Competencies or Practice Behaviors:
- EP 2.1.3c   Demonstrate effective oral and written communication in working with individuals, families, groups, organizations, communities, and colleagues
- EP 2.1.10a Substantively and affectively prepare for action with individuals, families, groups, organizations, and communities

Instructions:
A.   Review chapter 16 in the text prior to beginning this exercise.
B.   You can do this exercise with another classmate. Arbitrarily decide who will role-play the worker and who will role-play the client. The worker should interview the client to get the information necessary to fill out the face sheet displayed below. The face sheet is a type of standardized form which provides basic identifying information and is generally placed at the beginning of a client's file. This particular face sheet is for families applying to be foster families. In the role-play, the client should make up answers to the worker's questions.

Foster Home Licensing and Face Sheet[1]

Last Name	Address	Telephone
	City	County

Husband or Single Person | Wife

First Name   Birthdate | First Name   Birthdate

Race   Religion | Race   Religion

Occupation | Occupation

Work hours and phone | Work hours and phone

Ages of own children in home:

Boys

Girls

---

[1] This form is adapted from one used by the State of Wisconsin Department of Health and Social Services (DHSS). Printed with permission of the Wisconsin DHSS, 1 West Wilson, Madison, WI.

```
List names and ages of foster children now in home _____
_____
Schools foster child might attend _____
_____
Special child care skills _____
_____
License Information:  # of children _____        Sex of children _____
Age of children _____ Other limitations _____
Description of Home: total # of rooms _____    Number of bedrooms _____
Occupants in Home: Number of adults _____    Number of own children ____
        Number of other persons (excluding foster children) _____
Agency responsible for licensing _____
Agency responsible for supervision _____
        Date of License:  From _____ To _____
Submitted by _____    _____
                        Worker                          Date
Approved by _____
```

C.   After about fifteen minutes, your instructor will end the role play and begin a class discussion focusing on the following questions and issues:

1.   How easy or difficult did the workers find filling out the form?

2.   Were there any areas on the form which you found difficult to fill in? If so, what were they and why were they difficult?

3.   What other types of standardized forms might you have to use in real practice?

Focus Competencies or Practice Behaviors:

- EP 2.1.1d   Demonstrate professional demeanor in behavior, appearance, and communication
- EP 2.1.3a   Distinguish, appraise, and integrate multiple sources of knowledge, including research-based knowledge and practice wisdom
- EP 2.1.3c   Demonstrate effective oral and written communication in working with individuals, families, groups, organizations, communities, and colleagues
- EP 2.1.10a Substantively and affectively prepare for action with individuals, families, groups, organizations, and communities

Instructions:

A. Review chapter 16 in the text prior to beginning this exercise.

B. Choose a person you would like to interview. This could be a friend, a relative, or an acquaintance. Explain to the person that social histories reflect the important aspects of an individual's development and help social workers assess the nature of client's problems. Feel free to show the person the social history form. The person needs to know exactly what to expect, especially since you will be asking some personal questions about his or her life.

C. As you interview, fill out the social history form provided below. Remember that the purpose is not to investigate every minute detail of a person's life, but rather to gain a generalized understanding of what's most significant. In a real practice situation, you would be especially attuned to information relating to and clarifying the individual's designated problem. You would also pay special attention to identifying and evaluating the client's strengths.

Social History Format[2]

Name _____   D.O.B. _____
Address: _____
Telephone: _____
School and Grade: _____
Place of Birth: _____
Religion: _____

Outline for Social History

I.   Family Composition:
     (Note if any parent or sibling is deceased and date)

     Natural Father: _____   D.O.B. _____
     Address:
     Occupation:
     Religion:

---

[2] Adapted from the form "Outline for Social History." This material is printed with permission of the Community Human Services Department, Waukesha County, 500 Riverview Ave., Waukesha, WI 53188.

Stepfather: (if appropriate)   D.O.B. _____
Address:
Occupation:
Religion:

Natural Mother: D.O.B. _____
Address:
Occupation:
Religion:

Stepmother: D.O.B. _____
Address:
Occupation:
Religion:

Siblings:
Name, d.o.b., school, and grade. List all siblings, including those out of home, and current situation. If client or siblings are living with others, state names, addresses, and relationship.

II.   Child Under Consideration
      Describe personality and physical characteristics.

III. Reason for Referral:
      Short statement about immediate concern, current situation, and by whom referred. Parent's and child's attitudes about possible placement outside the home.

IV.   Family Background:

      A.   Mother:
            1.   Relationship to each of her parents; relationship between
                  her parents; evidence of emotional disturbance in family.

            2.   Mother's educational and vocational history.

234

3.   Medical history if pertinent.

4.   Previous marriages, with significant details.

5.   History of her courting and marriage, including feelings about marriage and children.

B.   <u>Father:</u>

1.   Relationship to each of his parents; relationship between his parents; evidence of emotional disturbance in family.

2.   Father's educational and vocational history.

3.   Medical history if pertinent.

4.   Previous marriages, with significant details.

5.   History of his courting and marriage, including feelings about marriage and children.

C.   <u>Family Development:</u>

1.   <u>Parental Relationships:</u>
Describe parental relationships, who disciplines whom and how, nature of and reasons for conflicts, family attitude toward current situation, family's financial situation and community involvement, family involvement with law enforcement and mental health agencies. What do you see happening in the family and why? This section should contain a historical perspective and comment on the past as well as the present.

2.   <u>Sibling Relationships:</u>
Describe child's relationship with each sibling; to whom child is closest and from whom most alienated; and reaction to birth of next youngest sibling. Describe any specific problems or emotional difficulties siblings in family have or have had in the past and how handled by parents.

3.   <u>Other Significant Adults:</u>
Ex-grandparents, aunts, uncles, neighbors, teachers. Indicate who and type of relationship and when it began.

4.   <u>Environment:</u>
Significance of neighborhoods family has lived in and their dwellings.

V.   <u>Personal History of Child:</u>

A.   <u>Developmental Data:</u>
Parental relationship during pregnancy, reaction to pregnancy, preferred sex, mother's health (signs of miscarriage, emotional state, significant use or abuse of drugs or alcohol).

<u>Birth:</u>
Delivery: premature or full term spontaneous? Physical condition of mother and child, length of hospital stay.

Early Months:

Note any changes in mother's physical or emotional health. Any difficulties in adjusting to the home—was it stable at this time? Did child have colic or other problems? Was child breast or bottle fed? Any feeding difficulties? Note changes in any caretakers and significant losses.

Later Months and Toddler Stage:

Note ages at which child walked, talked, and was toilet trained. Note any difficulties re: sleep and eating patterns.

Coordination and Motor Pattern:

A general statement as well as noting any hyperactivity, sluggishness, head or body rocking, random or unorganized activity.

Parents' feelings regarding above and how they attempted to handle any difficulties.

B.   ### Personality and Social Growth:

Responsiveness: Did child like to be held or did he or she withdraw from people? Did the child play with adults and/or children? Did he or she play in group or prefer to play alone?

Relationships: Describe relationship with each parent as related by both parents and child. Explore any differences. What about relationships with siblings?

Separations from either or both parents: When, why, how long? Note also parental and child response toward separating to attend school.

Describe child's outstanding traits and fears if any, e.g., is the child happy, sullen, stubborn, dependent, independent? Does she or he have any persistent fears, phobias, or compulsions?

Discipline: How and by whom? How have parents and child reacted to it?

Sexual development: Amount of sex education. Who provided? Unusual behavior or preoccupations; kind of questions or curiosity displayed; masturbation; parental response.

C.   Medical History:
Any illness or disease suffered; injuries, falls, high fevers, convulsions, fainting or other spells, allergies or other somatic disturbances; child and parent reactions. Also any hospitalization history. Touch on any previous treatment for current problems, previous psychiatric treatment. Type and extent of drug usage, if any.

Birth disfigurements, speech defects, enuresis, handicaps.

Present health.

D.   Educational Experiences:
Schools and years attended, achievement, testing dates done by schools, M-Team reports, interpersonal relationships of child; parents' relationship with school systems, extra-curricular activities.

Psychological and psychiatric evaluations—previous referrals, contacts, treatment, and progress.

E.   Employment Experience:

VI.   Previous Treatment:
Prior placements and services, successful completion or failure of services and/or placements.

Substantiate that care and services that would permit the child to remain at home have been investigated and considered and are not available or likely to become available within a reasonable time to meet the needs of the child.

A.   What alternatives to the plan are available?

B.   What alternatives have been explored?

C.   Why are explored alternatives not appropriate?

D.   Discuss objectives of rehabilitation, treatment, and care.

VII.   <u>Reference Sources:</u>

Label and date interviews, reports, letters used to complete the social history.

Date: _____

Prepared by: _____

(Social Worker)

Approved by: _____

(Supervisor)

SS-153 (Rev. '82)

D.   Turn your completed social history in to your instructor for feedback and grading.

Competencies/Practice Behaviors Exercise 16.3
Writing a Memo

Focus Competencies or Practice Behaviors:
- EP 2.1.1d   Demonstrate professional demeanor in behavior, appearance, and communication
- EP 2.1.3c   Demonstrate effective oral and written communication in working with individuals, families, groups, organizations, communities, and colleagues
- EP 2.1.10b Use empathy and other interpersonal skills
- EP 2.1.10h Initiate actions to achieve organizational goals

Instructions:
A.   Prior to beginning this exercise, review chapter 16, especially the material on memos.
B.   Read the following situation:

Case Situation

You are a social worker for Oconomowoc County Social Services. You've been with the agency for a little over a year. All employees are supposed to have an annual performance review. Only workers whose supervisors submit a positive review of the workers' performance will receive a raise in salary for the next year.

You have what you consider an adequate relationship with your supervisor, Chuck Norris. You feel he's neither especially helpful nor knowledgeable. However, he's relatively easy going and lets you do your job "in peace." You get the help and consultation you need from your colleagues and other supervisors in the agency.

The problem is that you've asked Chuck three times, the last in writing, when he has time to sit down with you and do your review. Each time he passed off your request casually and said he didn't have time. The last time you approached him you even subtly reminded him that performance reviews are due within the next week or two. You know that if he doesn't do your review, you won't get a raise next year. You feel you really worked hard this year and really need that raise. Your '97 Dodge Neon is on its last legs and you can't handle the monthly payments for a new car without a raise.

You don't think Chuck really likes to do performance reviews. In fact, you question his overall professional competence. You also don't think he's going to get around to doing your review. You feel that reminding him again would be useless.

You decide that the only way to handle the situation is to contact Chuck's supervisor, Ethyl Mettelschmerz, who is the agency's assistant director. She's very busy with her own responsibilities. You feel the only way to get her attention is to send her a memo about the situation.

You know you must choose your words carefully. You must get your point across without crucifying Chuck. You also don't want to sound angry. You want to state the facts as calmly and nonjudgmentally as possible. You realize that you will have to live with Chuck as your supervisor next year, too.

You write the memo . . .

C. Take fifteen minutes and write a memo to Ethyl about the situation, and then answer the following questions:

1. What did you write in your memo?

2. What was most difficult about writing the memo?

3. Did you follow the format provided in the text?

4. What did you learn about writing memos from this exercise?

Competencies/Practice Behaviors Exercise 16.4
Writing Professional Letters

Focus Competencies or Practice Behaviors:

- EP 2.1.1d Demonstrate professional demeanor in behavior, appearance, and communication
- EP 2.1.3c Demonstrate effective oral and written communication in working with individuals, families, groups, organizations, communities, and colleagues
- EP 2.1.10b Use empathy and other interpersonal skills
- EP 2.1.10j Help clients resolve problems

Instructions:

A. Prior to beginning the exercise, review chapter 16, especially the section about writing letters.
B. Read the following:

Case Situation

You are a Case Manager for a local family services agency. A major part of your job is to place young adults with cognitive disabilities in the community and coordinate the supportive services for them.

One of the clients you've recently placed in her own apartment is Holly Wood, twenty-three. She is an attractive, well-dressed young woman who can read at a fifth-grade level. She is proud of her full-time job as a file clerk at a nearby hospital. Although many people with higher intellectual abilities might find this job dull, Holly performs the repetitive tasks involved responsibly and conscientiously. Holly's social life primarily involves a "social club" she belongs to, made up of other developmentally disabled people of similar ability. Group activities are supervised by the family services agency staff.

The problem is that Holly's mother, Mrs. DeHavilland, calls you and screams irately that she will not allow Holly to date "those boys" in the social club. She feels strongly that Holly is not able to handle such activities and that she might get involved in "that sex thing."

In fact, Holly has dated two men in the club. One date involved a movie and pizza, and the other a baseball game. Although Holly has not as yet gotten serious about any of the men in the club, the potential is certainly there.

Your agency's philosophy is that clients have the right to make their own decisions and to develop relationships just as "normal" people do. Some of the supportive services you coordinate for clients include sex education and counseling to develop responsible decision-making skills. Clients are encouraged and helped to live "normal" lives. They participate in "normal" activities and make "normal" mistakes.

You need to write a letter to Mrs. DeHavilland and tell her in a civil and supportive yet firm way that Holly has the right to make her own decisions. You can stress the help the agency is providing her. You can also emphasize your appreciation for Mrs. DeHavilland's concern about and love for Holly.

C. Using the suggestions for letter writing provided in the text, take fifteen minutes to write the letter mentioned in the vignette above.

D. Answer the following questions:

1. What did you write in your letter?

2. What specific phrases did you choose to get your various points across?

3. To what extent did you follow the format and suggestions provided in the text?

4. What did you find most difficult about writing the letter?

5. What did you learn about letter writing from this experience?

Focus Competencies or Practice Behaviors:

- EP 2.1.1d   Demonstrate professional demeanor in behavior, appearance, and communication
- EP 2.1.1f   Use supervision and consultation
- EP 2.1.3a   Distinguish, appraise, and integrate multiple sources of knowledge, including research-based knowledge and practice wisdom
- EP 2.1.3c   Demonstrate effective oral and written communication in working with individuals, families, groups, organizations, communities, and colleagues
- EP 2.1.10a Substantively and affectively prepare for action with individuals, families, groups, organizations, and communities
- EP 2.1.10b Use empathy and other interpersonal skills
- EP 2.1.10d Collect, organize, and interpret client data

Instructions:

A.   Review chapter 16 in the text prior to beginning this exercise, especially pertaining to writing a social history.

B.   The instructor will ask for volunteers to role-play clients, each with separate issues. Some may role-play a family, some may be a lesbian couple with issues over their child, or any other type of issue that a social worker may see at intake.

C.   Each situation will also need a social worker to record the social history. Because of the time involved, you will only be recording the following sections of the social history.

D.   Remember that the purpose is not to investigate every minute detail of a person's life, but rather to gain a generalized understanding of what's most significant. In a real practice situation, you would be especially attuned to information relating to and clarifying the individual's designated problem. You would also pay special attention to identifying and evaluating the client's strengths.

Social History Format[2]

Name _____   D.O.B. _____
Address: _____
Telephone: _____
School and Grade: _____
Place of Birth: _____
Religion: _____

Outline for Social History

I.   Family Composition:
        (Note if any parent or sibling is deceased and date)

        Natural Father: D.O.B. _____

---

[2] Adapted from the form "Outline for Social History." This material is printed with permission of the Community Human Services Department, Waukesha County, 500 Riverview Ave., Waukesha, WI 53188.

Stepfather: (if appropriate)   D.O.B. _____

Natural Mother: D.O.B. _____

Stepmother: D.O.B. _____

Siblings:
List all siblings, including those out of home, and current situation.

II.   Person Under Consideration:
Describe personality and physical characteristics.

III.   Reason for Referral:
Short statement about immediate concern, current situation, and by whom referred. Parent's and child's attitudes about possible placement outside the home.

1.   Family Development:
Describe parental relationships, who disciplines whom and how, nature of and reasons for conflicts, family attitude toward current situation, family's financial situation and community involvement, family involvement with law enforcement and mental health agencies. What do you see happening in the family and why? This section should contain a historical perspective and comment on the past as well as the present.

2.   Sibling Relationships:
Describe child's relationship with each sibling; to whom child is closest and from whom most alienated; and reaction to birth of next youngest sibling. Describe any specific problems or emotional difficulties siblings in family have or have had in the past and how handled by parents.

3.   Other Significant Adults:
Ex-grandparents, aunts, uncles, neighbors, teachers. Indicate who and type of relationship and when it began.

E.   Answer the following questions (pertaining to the role you played):

1.   How easy or difficult did the workers find filling out the form?

2.   Were there any areas on the form which you found difficult to fill in? If so, what were they and why were they difficult?

3. If you were a client, what were your feelings about answering the questions? Did you feel vulnerable or were you comfortable? Explain.

4. Did you feel that the worker was empathic and practiced professional communication and skills? What could have been done differently?

Chapter 16 Competencies/Practice Behaviors Exercises Assessment:

Name: _____ **Date:** _____

Supervisor's Name: _____

Focus Competencies/Practice Behaviors:

- EP 2.1.1d   Demonstrate professional demeanor in behavior, appearance, and communication
- EP 2.1.1f   Use supervision and consultation
- EP 2.1.3a   Distinguish, appraise, and integrate multiple sources of knowledge, including research-based knowledge and practice wisdom
- EP 2.1.3c   Demonstrate effective oral and written communication in working with individuals, families, groups, organizations, communities, and colleagues
- EP 2.1.10a   Substantively and affectively prepare for action with individuals, families, groups, organizations, and communities
- EP 2.1.10b   Use empathy and other interpersonal skills
- EP 2.1.10h   Initiate actions to achieve organizational goals
- EP 2.1.10j   Help clients resolve problems

Instructions:

A.   Evaluate your work or your partner's work in the Focus Competencies/Practice Behaviors by completing the Competencies/Practice Behaviors Assessment form below

B.   What other Competencies/Practice Behaviors did you use to complete these Exercises? Be sure to record them in your assessments

1.	I have attained this competency/practice behavior (in the range of 81 to 100%)
2.	I have largely attained this competency/practice behavior (in the range of 61 to 80%)
3.	I have partially attained this competency/practice behavior (in the range of 41 to 60%)
4.	I have made a little progress in attaining this competency/practice behavior (in the range of 21 to 40%)
5.	I have made almost no progress in attaining this competency/practice behavior (in the range of 0 to 20%)

EPAS 2008 Core Competencies & Core Practice Behaviors	Student Self Assessment						Evaluator Feedback
Student and Evaluator Assessment Scale and Comments	0	1	2	3	4	5	**Agree/Disagree/Comments**
EP 2.1.1 Identify as a Professional Social Worker and Conduct Oneself Accordingly:							
a. Advocate for client access to the services of social work							
b. Practice personal reflection and self-correction to assure continual professional development							
c. Attend to professional roles and boundaries							
d. Demonstrate professional demeanor in behavior, appearance, and communication							
e. Engage in career-long learning							
f. Use supervision and consultation							
EP 2.1.2 Apply Social Work Ethical Principles to Guide Professional Practice:							
a. Recognize and manage personal values in a way that allows professional values to guide practice							
b. Make ethical decisions by applying NASW Code of Ethics and, as applicable, of the							

249

IFSW/IASSW Ethics in Social Work, Statement of Principles					
c. Tolerate ambiguity in resolving ethical conflicts					
d. Apply strategies of ethical reasoning to arrive at principled decisions					
EP 2.1.3 Apply Critical Thinking to Inform and Communicate Professional Judgments:					
a. Distinguish, appraise, and integrate multiple sources of knowledge, including research-based knowledge and practice wisdom					
b. Analyze models of assessment, prevention, intervention, and evaluation					
c. Demonstrate effective oral and written communication in working with individuals, families, groups, organizations, communities, and colleagues					
EP 2.1.4 Engage Diversity and Difference in Practice:					
a. Recognize the extent to which a culture's structures and values may oppress, marginalize, alienate, or create or enhance privilege and power					
b. Gain sufficient self-awareness to eliminate the influence of personal biases and values in working with diverse groups					
c. Recognize and communicate their understanding of the importance of difference in shaping life experiences					
d. View themselves as learners and engage those with whom they work as informants					
EP 2.1.5 Advance Human Rights and Social and Economic Justice:					
a. Understand forms and mechanisms of oppression and discrimination					
b. Advocate for human rights and social and economic justice					
c. Engage in practices that advance social and economic justice					
EP 2.1.6 Engage in Research-Informed Practice and Practice-Informed Research:					
a. Use practice experience to inform scientific inquiry					
b. Use research evidence to inform practice					
EP 2.1.7 Apply Knowledge of Human Behavior and the Social Environment:					
a. Utilize conceptual frameworks to guide the processes of assessment, intervention, and evaluation					
b. Critique and apply knowledge to understand person and environment					
EP 2.1.8 Engage in Policy Practice to Advance Social and Economic Well-Being and to Deliver Effective Social Work Services:					
a. Analyze, formulate, and advocate for policies that advance social well-being					
b. Collaborate with colleagues and clients for effective policy action					
EP 2.1.9 Respond to Contexts that Shape Practice:					
a. Continuously discover, appraise, and attend to changing locales, populations, scientific and technological developments, and emerging societal trends to provide relevant services					

250

b.	Provide leadership in promoting sustainable changes in service delivery and practice to improve the quality of social services							
EP 2.1.10 Engage, Assess, Intervene, and Evaluate with Individuals, Families, Groups, Organizations and Communities:								
a.	Substantively and affectively prepare for action with individuals, families, groups, organizations, and communities							
b.	Use empathy and other interpersonal skills							
c.	Develop a mutually agreed-on focus of work and desired outcomes							
d.	Collect, organize, and interpret client data							
e.	Assess client strengths and limitations							
f.	Develop mutually agreed-on intervention goals and objectives							
g.	Select appropriate intervention strategies							
h.	Initiate actions to achieve organizational goals							
i.	Implement prevention interventions that enhance client capacities							
j.	Help clients resolve problems							
k.	Negotiate, mediate, and advocate for clients							
l.	Facilitate transitions and endings							
m.	Critically analyze, monitor, and evaluate interventions							

Kirst-Ashman/Hull's *Understanding Generalist Practice, 6e and Competencies/Practice Behaviors Workbook* Aligned to EPAS 2008 Competencies and Practice Behaviors

Competencies and Practice Behaviors	Understanding Generalist Practice, 6e Chapters:	Practice Behaviors Workbook Practice Exercises:
2.1.1 Identify as a Professional Social Worker and Conduct Oneself Accordingly	4	4.3
a. Advocate for client access to the services of social work	2, 3, 4	4.4, 14.4
b. Practice personal reflection and self-correction to assure continual professional development	2, 8, 11, 16	1.1, 2.2, 9.1, 12.2, 13.1, 13.2, 13.5
c. Attend to professional roles and boundaries	1, 2, 3, 4, 5, 7, 11, 15	4.3, 4.4, 7.3, 9.5, 10.1, 10.2, 10.3, 10.4, 11.5, 11.6, 11.7, 11.9, 14.2, 15.1
d. Demonstrate professional demeanor in behavior, appearance, and communication	4, 10, 11, 14, 16	4.1, 4.2, 4.4, 7.3, 10.1, 10.2, 10.3, 10.4, 14.3, 14.4, 16.2, 16.3, 16.4, 16.5
e. Engage in career-long learning	2, 11, 12, 16	5.2
f. Use supervision and consultation	1, 3, 4, 8, 11, 16	4.4, 11.5, 11.6, 14.2, 16.5
2.1.2 Apply Social Work Ethical Principles to Guide Professional Practice	1, 4, 7, 11	
a. Recognize and manage personal values in a way that allows professional values to guide practice	9, 11	1.4, 2.3, 7.2, 11.1, 11.2, 11.3, 11.4, 11.5, 11.6, 11.7, 11.8, 11.9, 13.5, 14.4

b. Make ethical decisions by applying standards of the National Association of Social Workers Code of Ethics and, as applicable, of the International Federation of Social Workers/International Association of Schools of Social Work Ethics in Social Work, Statement of Principles	4, 8, 11, 15, 16	11.1, 11.2, 11.3, 11.4, 11.8, 11.9, 13.1, 13.6
c. Tolerate ambiguity in resolving ethical conflicts	11	1.4, 11.1, 11.2, 11.3, 11.4, 11.5, 11.6, 11.7, 11.8, 11.9
d. Apply strategies of ethical reasoning to arrive at principled decisions	11	1.4, 11.1, 11.2, 11.3, 11.4, 11.5, 11.6, 11.7, 11.8, 11.9
2.1.3 Apply Critical Thinking to Inform and Communicate Professional Judgments	1, 2, 3, 4, 5, 6, 7, 8, 9, 10, 11, 12, 13, 14, 15, 16	3.1, 3.2, 4.3, 5.1, 6.1, 6.2, 6.3, 8.1, 8.2, 8.3, 8.4, 12.3, 12.4, 14.1, 14.2, 14.3, 14.4, 15.1
a. Distinguish, appraise, and integrate multiple sources of knowledge, including research-based knowledge and practice wisdom	8, 11	9.3, 10.4, 16.2, 16.5
b. Analyze models of assessment, prevention, intervention, and evaluation	6, 8	7.3
c. Demonstrate effective oral and written communication in working with individuals, families, groups, organizations, communities, and colleagues	2, 4, 5, 11, 14, 16	4.1, 4.2, 4.4, 7.4, 9.5, 10.1, 10.2, 10.4, 11.9, 14.3, 16.1, 16.2, 16.3, 16.4, 16.5
2.1.4 Engage Diversity and Difference in Practice	1, 2, 5, 7, 9, 10, 11, 13	12.1, 12.2, 12.4, 13.1, 13.2, 13.3, 13.4, 13.5, 13.6
a. Recognize the extent to which a culture's structures and values may oppress, marginalize, alienate, or create or enhance privilege and power	2, 5, 6, 7, 8, 10, 11, 12, 13	

b. Gain sufficient self-awareness to eliminate the influence of personal biases and values in working with diverse groups	5, 7, 12, 13	7.2, 12.2, 13.1, 13.2, 13.5
c. Recognize and communicate their understanding of the importance of difference in shaping life experiences	8, 9, 12, 13	12.2, 12.3, 13.1, 13.2, 13.5
d. View themselves as learners and engage those with whom they work as informants;	12	13.5
2.1.5 Advance Human Rights and Social and Economic Justice	4, 5, 11, 13	
a. Understand forms and mechanisms of oppression and discrimination	10, 11, 12, 13	12.4, 13.2, 13.6
b. Advocate for human rights and social and economic justice	1, 3, 4, 10, 11, 13, 14	3.1, 4.4, 14.1
c. Engage in practices that advance social and economic justice	4, 10, 11, 13	
2.1.6 Engage in Research-Informed Practice and Practice-Informed Research	1, 3, 16	
a. Use practice experience to inform scientific inquiry	5, 8, 11, 16	
b. Use research evidence to inform practice	8, 10, 12, 16	12.1
2.1.7 Apply Knowledge of Human Behavior and the Social Environment	1	
a. Utilize conceptual frameworks to guide the process of assessment, intervention, and evaluation	1, 3, 4, 5, 7, 8, 9, 13	1.5, 1.6, 5.3, 7.1, 8.1, 8.2
b. Critique and apply knowledge to understand person and environment	5, 7, 9, 14	1.5, 1.6, 7.4, 9.1, 9.2, 9.4

254

2.1.8	**Engage in Policy Practice to Advance Social and Economic Well-Being and to Deliver Effective Social Work Services**	1, 3	3.1
a.	Analyze, formulate, and advocate for policies that advance social well-being	1, 4, 7, 10, 13	1.3, 9.3
b.	Collaborate with colleagues and clients for effective policy action	4, 11, 13	4.4, 14.4
2.1.9	**Respond to Contexts that Shape Practice**	4	
a.	Continuously discover, appraise, and attend to changing locales, populations, scientific and technological developments, and emerging societal trends to provide relevant services	10, 13, 16	9.3
b.	Provide leadership in promoting sustainable changes in service delivery and practice to improve the quality of social services	4, 11, 13	4.4
2.1.10	**Engage, Assess, Intervene, and Evaluate with Individuals, Families, Groups, Organizations and Communities**	1, 2, 3, 5, 6, 7, 10, 13, 16	3.3, 3.4, 5.1, 6.1
a.	Substantively and affectively prepare for action with individuals, families, groups, organizations, and communities	1, 2, 3, 7, 9, 10, 13, 16	1.2, 1.3, 2.7, 3.3, 7.1, 7.3, 7.4, 9.1, 9.4, 9.5, 10.1, 10.2, 10.3, 10.4, 11.9, 16.1, 16.2, 16.5
b.	Use empathy and other interpersonal skills	2, 4, 5, 7, 13	2.1, 2.2, 2.5, 2.6, 2.7, 7.3, 7.4, 9.5, 10.1, 10.2, 10.3, 10.4, 11.9, 16.3, 16.4, 16.5
c.	Develop a mutually agreed-on focus of work and desired outcomes.	5, 6, 7, 10, 13, 16	6.1, 6.2, 6.4, 7.3, 9.5, 10.1, 10.2, 10.3, 10.4, 11.9
d.	Collect, organize, and interpret client data	4, 5, 7, 9, 14, 16	2.4, 5.1, 7.3, 7.4, 9.2, 9.4, 10.1, 10.2, 10.3, 10.4, 11.9, 14.1, 16.5

e. Assess client strengths and limitations	1, 2, 5, 6, 7, 10, 12, 13, 14, 15, 16	5.3, 5.4, 6.1, 6.2, 7.3, 7.4, 9.2, 9.4, 9.5, 10.1, 10.2, 10.3, 10.4, 11.9, 12.4, 15.2, 15.3
f. Develop mutually agreed-on intervention goals and objectives	1, 5, 6, 7, 10, 15, 16	6.1, 6.2, 6.3, 6.4, 7.3, 7.4, 9.5, 10.1, 10.2, 10.3, 10.4, 11.9, 14.1, 15.1, 15.3
g. Select appropriate intervention strategies	6, 7, 10, 13, 14, 15, 16	1.2, 7.1, 7.4, 9.5, 10.1, 10.2, 10.3, 10.4, 11.9, 13.3, 13.4, 13.6, 14.1, 15.1
h. Initiate actions to achieve organizational goals	3, 4, 5, 8, 11, 16	16.3
i. Implement prevention interventions that enhance client capacities	6, 7, 8, 9, 10	
j. Help clients resolve problems	3, 7, 9, 10, 13	3.1, 7.3, 7.4, 9.5, 10.1, 10.2, 10.3, 10.4, 11.9, 16.4
k. Negotiate, mediate, and advocate for clients	2, 3, 4, 14	4.4, 14.4
l. Facilitate transitions and endings	1, 2, 8, 10, 11, 16	8.3
m. Critically analyze, monitor, and evaluate interventions	1, 4, 7, 8, 10, 15, 16	8.1, 8.2, 8.4, 15.4

256